PRAISE FOR *THE TR[*

MW00789287

The Trust Puzzle is a fast-paced summary of the ethics questions facing business today. Frank Bucaro helps leaders focus on what's important and keep the moral compass calibrated. This book is a reference that I can go back to again and again.

Matt Calabro
Chief Compliance Officer
Northern Trust Asset Management

With Bucaro's insights, experience and practical advice, solving your trust puzzle is no longer a mystery. He helps you find all the pieces and how to assemble them, to assure your success. Place your trust in Bucaro and his powerful principles, to achieve new levels of prosperity and fulfillment.

Jeff Blackman, J.D., CSP, CPAE
Bestselling Author of *Stop Whining! Start Selling!* and *Peak Your Profits!*

Trust Puzzle takes the guess work out of fostering an ethical organization. It provides tools and insights into sustaining ethics by helping the reader both question and develop their moral compass so they can be an effective leader. But this book is not only for organizational leaders; it can improve any individual. We all have leader roles in life – we lead our children, spouses, friends, family and sometimes even strangers. Any time an ethical situation arises, our decision on how to respond sets the tone for others. *Trust Puzzle* is spot on when it states "...people tend to listen with their eyes more than with their ears. What you do, says so much more than what you say." An excellent read for anyone searching to gain a better perspective of ethics!

Julie Rys-Sours
Compliance Officer
Together4Health

Frank Bucaro's new book, *The Trust Puzzle: How to keep your Company on the Ethical High Road* is all about values based and principled driven leadership. What I liked most are the examples, the wisdom and the applications he provides.

The book starts off with a quote from Warren Buffett, "It takes 20 years to build a reputation and five minutes to ruin it. If you think about that, you'll do things differently." So here's my advice to you, think about that as you read Frank's book.

Frank provides a list of five leadership virtues that can make a real difference. For me, this alone was worth the price of the book. One of the things you get throughout Frank's book are little pearls of wisdom. He's constantly asking questions, that get you thinking and may even keep you up at night. For example, Reputation: is the one you have the one you want?

And here's another one, would you hire a whistle blower? What a question to contemplate!

He also talks about developing a moral compass. Of course that's easy to say and hard to do. I've known Frank for 30 years. He has a genuine moral compass unlike any other person I've known in my lifetime.

Get the book. Read the book. Enjoy the experience.

Jim Meisenheimer
Author of seven books - Amazon Best Selling Author
Creator Knockout Selling Training Programs
Publisher of The No-Brainer Selling Tips BLOG
Creator of The Surefire Selling Results Pyramid
Former Vice President of Sales and Marketing for Baxter International

Having known Frank for many years as a passionate and uncompromising ethics champion, I am truly excited to see his book published. What sets Frank apart from an army of bland commercial ethicists is his true commitment, passion, gravitas and authenticity combined with leader qualities and excellent communication skills. And his book *The Trust Puzzle* lets you feel that.

For someone like me coming from Russia whose social cohesion is under a lot of strain due to low trust within society and towards institutions, I find Frank's book to be of tremendous value to myself as an ethics practitioner. There are many takeaways and nuggets in his book, which I find precious for my own hobbit mission, because Frank's insights and observations are of holistic and universal nature. In the realm of business ethics his contribution to painful restoration of the healthy fabric of trust scorched by corporate misbehavior and Wall Street scandals rests on the lessons drawn from interactions with many senior execs. Those observations Frank forged into practical ways to recalibrate today's leaders' moral compass. This context makes it easier for business folks to read them and relate to. Even for the ones already afflicted by compliance fatigue.

Anatoly Yakorev
Director
Center for Business Ethics & Compliance CBEC
International University in Moscow

Frank Bucaro's *The Trust Puzzle* is essential reading for C-suite executives, managers and employees at all levels of an organization, and even job applicants who want to go above and beyond what most candidates discuss during job interviews (more on that in a moment).

Bucaro is a respected thought leader in business ethics and an in-demand keynote speaker to leading companies in the U.S. and beyond. I know him personally, and I can tell you that he embodies the qualities of high-character that he discusses in *The Trust Puzzle*.

Yes, CEOs and other C-suite executives will benefit from this book. As one chapter has it, "Trust Is Everything, for Without It You Have Nothing!" But it would be a grave mistake if only the people at the highest level of an organization were to read Bucaro's book.

Mid-level managers and employees in other positions will learn the difference between ethics and compliance, the reason why leadership should exist at all levels of an organization, and the high cost of failing to take ethics seriously.

Savvy people who want to land a plum job would do well to mine "The Trust Puzzle" for its insights into responsible corporate behavior. When the interviewer asks the inevitable, "Is there a question I should have asked you but didn't?," a smart job candidate who wants to move ahead of the pack should ask about the corporate culture that Bucaro discusses in this book. What are the company's values, and how are they enforced or emphasized? What would the interviewer like to see added to the company's Code of Conduct? What changes in the corporate culture would you, the interviewer, like to see? This last question opens the door for the candidate to say, "I can help you with that. Here's how..."

I respect Frank Bucaro, I value his work, and I encourage you to read *The Trust Puzzle* and make it mandatory reading for your next corporate retreat (and then hire Frank to facilitate a discussion about it).

Note: I have no financial interest in this book or in Frank's speaking engagements. I just believe in him, his message,

Bruce Weinstein
Author of *The Good Ones: Ten Crucial Qualities of High-Character Employees*

First, I'm a bit of a snob when it comes to attesting on the works of others. I'm an author, a Regional Vice-President of a national mortgage company as well as a practicing attorney. You could say that this book isn't about ethics, but rather about leadership. Because truly great leaders actually lead through serving and modeling. And one of the most important ingredients is ethics.

Here's the issue that most people miss. Many people think that they're leaders because they have people "reporting" to them. Unfortunately, most "leaders" aren't really leaders at all and, as a result, the ethics that they employ are questionable at best.

Through *The Trust Puzzle* Frank tells the reader what it takes to be great... without sacrificing ethics. Rather, to be a great leader you need great ethics. After all, others model their behavior after on your actions.

Frank doesn't mince words. It's a easy read that many may put down only because their own ethics may come into question when they look inside. However, for those who truly want to be the best, and model like the best, there is nothing better than a deep look inward. Personally, I felt a bit uncomfortable during certain parts of the book as *The Trust Puzzle* made me look deeper inside than I usually would. I like what I came away with. I also found ways that I can improve.

Frank has a way with personal anecdotes and stories that will challenge even the best of us.

Having said all of that...the book is a very easy read. It's broken into 4 parts that will take through the journey that you need to see internally and within your business or for the group of leaders you may serve...or even those who lead others.

You can't grow anything great or create any meaningful legacies without Ethics. Frank's book, *The Trust Puzzle*, is a must for you or your company.

And no...I wasn't paid for this review. I'm just passionate about leadership and legacy creation. A Ethics Must! Thanks Frank.

Jerome L. Bettag
Regional Vice President
Cherry Creek Mortgage

THE TRUST PUZZLE

THE TRUST PUZZLE:

How to Keep Your Company on the Ethical High Road

by Frank C. Bucaro CSP, CPAE

ISBN: 978-1-946229-89-2

Books and more that make the world better!

www.networlding.com

THE TRUST PUZZLE

How to Keep Your Company on the Ethical High Road

FRANK C. BUCARO CSP, CPAE

TABLE OF CONTENTS

INTRODUCTION

Welcome to this series focusing on values-based and princi-ple-driven leadership. After 30 years as a professional speaker and author and having worked in just about every industry, I have compiled a comprehensive series of examples, insights, theories, wisdom and applications to the issue of values-based leadership development. Although not an exhaustive series in itself, it will challenge you, inspire you and give you many "Ah-ha" moments, when implemented, that can change your workplace environment.

To help you get the most out of the content, I've broken down the series into fast-paced, tangible, easy-to-read segments so you can immediately implement your learnings with your staff, employees and co-workers.

> "Morale filters down. It never filters up.
> People listen with their eyes."

What Are Ethics?

Ask ten business leaders what "business ethics" means and why it's important, and you'll get ten different answers. Why? Because most people equate ethics with the religious or professional codes that matter most to them. They think of things like the ten commandments, or the Hippocratic Oath (do no harm), or something more mainstream like the "Golden Rule" where we "do unto others like we'd like them to do unto us." Most of us rely on our culture, or that of society, for defining both our personal and professional ethics. But what are ethics, and is there a difference between personal and professional ethics?

The short definition is, "Ethics are the **norms for conduct** that distinguish between acceptable and unacceptable behavior in a given society." For instance, in some countries it's considered acceptable behavior to borrow someone's property, even if they are a stranger, if you need it. Of course you return it when you're finished. In the United States we ask before borrowing property, otherwise the person we're borrowing it from would assume we're stealing it. If this sounds unbelievable, consider office environments. Do people believe it is "okay" to go through your drawers and files for office supplies or folders? Does your spouse go through your wallet, phone or bag? Depending on your family culture this may or may not be okay.

So, ethics, for the purpose of this book, are about the norms that distinguish acceptable and unacceptable behavior in the workplace, and particularly among our leaders, managers and bosses.

Following are the five sections and an intro to each:

1. **Grow a Good Reputation.** Think of a time when someone you know succeeded, failed, or was singled out for their reputation, one in a good way, one in a not-so-good way. How have you seen reputation hurt or help someone? This section will explore these questions.

2. **Build Trust and Loyalty.** Even with people who are unethical, trust and loyalty to the culture are important qualities. As the saying goes, "there's honor among thieves." Think of a time when trust and loyalty impressed a client, saved the day, or made a difference.

3. **Develop a Moral Compass.** It's easy to drift and get lost when you're in the woods, and not checking or using your compass correctly. Think of a time when someone looked up and realized they'd lost their way ethically, maybe by following the crowd, trying to please a new boss, taking on a new job or position and trying to fit in.

4. **Create Accountable Leadership.** Being accountable is easy when things are going well, but what
   about a time when things didn't go so well and being
   accountable meant someone had to accept the hit for
   team members who really screwed things up. What
   was that like? What happened after the leader got
   blasted for something he didn't do personally, but
   was responsible for. I can think of a true story about
   a Navy Seal whose failure cost a man his life. He just
   published a new book about it, and he details how he
   had to step up to a team of officers and be accountable. He was damn lucky more Seals weren't killed in
   the "friendly fire" episode. Good story. Book is called
   "Extreme Ownership." You can read the opening
   chapter/story by clicking on the "See inside" feature
   on Amazon.

5. **Practice Stewardship.** Read the section on this
   and then think about examples of people who have
   been good stewards, for example, financial planners
   or anyone with a fiduciary responsibility.

6. **What's Next?** It's one thing to read a book, think
   about it. Speculate on "what if" and even talk about
   your own "remember when…" examples. But what are
   you going to *do* about it? Have you done a self-inven-
   tory? Have you considered how to share what you've

learned with your team? Are you ready to create a plan for your next steps?

How to Benefit Most from This Book

The impetus for this book is the ongoing ethics issues still occurring in business. After researching and speaking to many companies on ethical leadership, I've narrowed the possible solutions to the prevention and promotion of five key components to help keep companies and their people on the ethical "high road." It is my hope that many of these key ideas, insights, and techniques will be of value to you and your people to help maintain a strong ethical culture and environment.

I find that, more and more, people just don't have time to read a lot today in this very content-deluged world. That's why I have purposefully written shorter, yet still very relevant chapters, that focus on a variety of ethics issues. You can choose to read this entire book at once or move through it much more slowly, taking time, perhaps, daily, to read a chapter and then use it as a lesson-for-the-day to be juxtaposed against the work you do and those with whom you interact. Any way you decide to proceed should help you take the insights you develop and then use them to help lead a more ethically focused life, inside and outside your work environment. I wish you a good journey!

SECTION ONE
Grow a Good Reputation

"It takes 20 years to build a reputation and five minutes to ruin it. If you think about that, you'll do things differently."

~ WARREN BUFFET

Reputation is what people think of you, and what traits and characteristics they associate with you. At its core, it's a measure of how much people trust you. Your reputation can take you farther than your money or resources, or it can block access to resources and opportunities no matter how much money you have. Reputation is a resource you should take as seriously, or more so, than your entire business. You can quickly rebuild your business if it fails. It takes years, decades even, to rebuild your reputation. And like Warren Buffet said, "It only takes five minutes to ruin a reputation."

Let's look at what goes into creating a strong reputation, beginning with Conscience.

What Happened to Conscience and Accountability?

"I believe that every large institution, whether
it's company, a government or a university
needs to have a conscience. The conscience
won't have the answer to every question, but the
conscience is a voice that needs to be heard."

~ BRAD SMITH OF MICROSOFT

Aristotle stated: "We are what we do." It is not our words that define our morals or conscience. It is our actions.

Conscience, that inner voice of reason that tells us when something is right or wrong, needs to be the discerning factor in decision making. However, this very basic trait is lacking in many institutions and people. Just watch the news or read a newspaper. From the marketplace to universities, from Wall Street to professional sports, *where* is conscience? It tells us a lot that conscience is so rare that when we see it, particularly if the media sees it, the event and the person displaying the conscientious acts are labeled "heroes" and are celebrated for what should be a common life skill — doing the right thing for the right reason. Why are we so surprised when someone does that? Could it be that the word "right" is too easily interpreted?

Is what's right, the same as what's legal? Is what's right, the same as what is ethical or moral?

Why is it that the concept of conscience is rarely referenced or emphasized?

Aquinas defined conscience as an act of determining that which I ought to do or not to do or that I was right or wrong in performing that action. That said, Aquinas stated there are two obligations in forming a conscience:

1. Must be objectively educated
2. Well informed

Aquinas presumes three key concepts are integral in his definition:

1. Analyzing in advance of what one ought to do. This can only happen if one knows and has internalized in advance what one's values, morals and ethics are, or what I call one's "line in the sand."
2. Taking the time, energy and effort to seriously reflect and evaluate the consequences of one's decision were worth it and if not what to do in the future to avoid the same mistake.

3. Nowhere is it implied that one should try to avoid paying the price for the decision.

What role does conscience play in discerning compliance issues? What role does conscience play in the courtroom, in corporations, education, etc.?

Does development of conscience come from family, community, society, religion, academics or??

If we can't pinpoint where and when conscience develops, then, like it or not, it falls on the business organization to do its best to facilitate the recognition, and necessity for conscience development, based on the organization's values, mission, ethics.

Therefore, the development of one's conscience needs to be a foundational principle and activity of any ethics training initiative, leadership development training or in just building a corporate environment of trust.

The real issue is, who or what organization will step up and take this ethical stance and challenge? The answer is, "every organization needs to step up." This should be a foundational concept and the very base of every culture, no matter what the organization or the company. So why isn't it? For many reasons. Let's start at the top. All conscience and culture flows downhill, as does all lack of conscience and all corrupt company culture. Conscience begins with the boss.

Why Don't Companies Fire Bad Bosses?

In a recent INC. magazine, there was an article titled: *Jerk Alert: The Real Cost of Bad Bosses.*[1]

In this article, the research revealed:

- 65% of employees say they'd take a new boss over a raise.
- Three out of every four employees report that their boss is the worst and most stressful part of their job.
- Bad bosses not only make employees unhappy—they make workers unhealthy as well.

So why aren't these people fired, and who condones this type of leadership?

Ethically speaking, how can a company keep these bosses, who can cause morale issues, ethics issues, productivity issues, compliance issues and employee turnover, on board? More

---

1   Ouimet, Maeghan. *"The Real Productivity Killer: Jerks."* Inc. n.d. Web. Accessed 20 December 2015. <http://www.inc.com/maeghan-ouimet/real-cost-bad-bosses.html>

importantly, what is the "cost" to the company and to employee morale for keeping these "bad" bosses?

Human resources, the board, and even C-suite executives and their peers have to know that these supervisors, managers and bosses are ineffective, and yet keeping them says what to the rest of the company that aren't jerks?

There are enough issues to deal with in a business, without keeping bosses that tend to be a "cancer" growing within. If we can be in a "preventive maintenance" mode in the healthcare industry, why not in all companies?

The "powers that be" need to be like cancer surgeons. A good doctor can't leave a cancerous tumor alone. They have to cut it out for the good of the body, (i.e. the organization). To condone this behavior, whether passively or actively, is a recipe for disaster. But wait, there's more!

According to Inc's infographic, 30,000 managers and employees polled considered the five top "bad boss flaws" not as something they did, but what they didn't do. These bad bosses:

1. Failed to inspire.

2. Accepted mediocrity.

3. Lacked clear vision and direction.

4. Were unable to collaborate (work well with others) and be a team player.

5. Failed to walk the talk.

Let's examine these five top flaws a little closer and shift the focus to their ethical implications.

If the above five flaws are standard for a bad boss, then:

1. What are the odds that ethics is a valued priority?

Remember, ethics is about how we treat others and how we act, based upon accepted norms of the culture or workplace we're in. If the company adheres to society's ethics, which are different from the company's ethics, there will be a schism, or inconsistency among managers, bosses and employees. Ethics will be a valued priority, but whose ethics? If the message from the top is, "Don't rock the boat," but the ethics of your culture or employees is "Follow the Golden Rule," then you're going to have issues.

2. What good would an organization's commitment to ethics do?

Like any good rule, boundary or standard of behavior, those expected to follow them must know that the rule, boundary or standards are enforced. They must believe that violating the ethical standards will result in sanctions or punishment, and that following them is rewarded.

3. How does an organization develop an "environment of trust" with this type of leadership?

The truth is, unless there is a clearly defined and enforced commitment to an ethical standard, there is no "environment of trust."

4. Does the "CYA" attitude take precedence over values and ethics?

When a "CYA" attitude takes precedence over the professed company values and ethics, it not only disrupts the exchange between the unethical boss and his/her employees. it redefines the company values. As the old saying goes, "The weakest link defines the strength of the strongest chain."

5. If nothing is done about the "bad" bosses, what does that say about their immediate bosses?

Let's go back to the weakest link in the chain analogy. This analogy comes from the science of "Constraint Theory." That's right. It's not just a saying, it's a science. Constraint theory identifies the weakest link as a "bottleneck." In other words, it's where the flow of what the company does becomes bound up and stops flowing. The Theory of Constraints was created by Dr Eli Goldratt and was published in his 1984 book *"The Goal."* According to Goldratt:

> *"...organizational performance is dictated by constraints. These are restrictions that prevent an organization from maximizing its performance and reaching its goals. Constraints can involve people, supplies, information, equipment, or even policies, and can be internal or external to an organization. The theory says that every system, no matter how well it performs, has at least one constraint that limits its performance – this is the system's "weakest link." The theory also says that a system can have only one constraint at a time, and that other areas of weakness are "non-constraints" until they become the weakest link."*[2]

Unfortunately, what this says about their bosses is that the entire managerial team has ethical issues. Maybe only one person is conspicuously flaunting the lack of ethics, but the entire chain is poisoned. It's like discovering a small hole and one termite crawling around it. On the surface the problem appears to be the one termite, but in reality the entire foundation is rotted.

---

2   Mind Tool Team. "The Theory of Constraints". n.d. Web. Accessed 20 December 2015. <https://www.mindtools.com/pages/article/toc.htm>

6. What are the effects of these "flaws" on the employee's, morale, customers, vendors or suppliers?

Ask the unethical boss what effect their behavior has on employees and they'll most likely shrug and say, "None." The truth is, workers with high moral standards are helpless against unethical behavior they notice in their bosses or peers. "An employee working for an employer or company with unethical, deceptive, and dishonest conduct will be directly affected physically and mentally, and may even come down with emotional and health related problems because of it,"[3] says SixSigmaOnline.org.[4]

Whether they can express their stress and the cause and effect of that stress or not, employees know a bad boss is bad for them.

According to The National Bureau of Economic Research, "Replacing a boss who is in the lower 10% of boss quality with one who is in the upper 10% of boss quality increases a team's

---

3   "The Consequence of Unethical Business Behavior." SixSigmaOnline. n.d. Web. Accessed 20 December 2015. <http://www.sixsigmaonline.org/six-sigma-training-certification-information/the-consequence-of-unethical-business-behavior/>

4   SixSigma is a strict set of techniques and tools for process improvement. It's also a disciplined, data-driven approach and methodology for eliminating defects (driving toward six standard deviations between the mean and the nearest specification limit) in any process – from manufacturing to transactional and from product to service.

total output by more than would adding one worker to a nine member team."[5]

7. What good would an organization's' commitment to ethics do if unethical bosses are allowed to go unchecked or punished?

8. How does an organization develop an environment of trust?

Why Don't Companies Fire "Bad" Bosses — Part 2

First of all, many thanks to all of you who offered your wisdom, experiences and insights for this study from Inc. magazine's article, *Jerk Alert*. In practically all of the responses no one was surprised at the findings. Many gave great personal examples, and nearly all felt "strained" hope that things would or could change.

So if these five flaws exist in your organization, what can be done? As I mentioned earlier, it seems to me that these five flaws are like cancer cells in that as soon as they are discovered they need to be destroyed before they spread.

The "powers that be" need to remove these bosses for the good of the organization.

5   Lazear, Edward P. Shaw, Kathryn L.. Stanton, Christopher T. "The Value of Bosses." National Bureau of Economic Research (NBER). NBER Working Paper. August 2013. Web. Accessed 20 December 2015. <http://www.nber.org/papers/w18317>

With all that said, let's re-examine these five top flaws and shift the focus to their ethical implications.

Ethical Decision Making and Buddha

Buddha once said: *"Mindfulness is the consideration of all implications of every decision you make." Mindfulness is the quality or practice of being conscious, and aware of things around us, including how those things make us feel, and how we think about how they affect us. This awareness can help us make wiser and more prudent decisions.*

Too bad so many organizations didn't embrace this wisdom *before* acting on the questionable compliance/ethical issues, many of which have now become public and subject to examination and debate. All of us, for that matter, need to embrace this "mindfulness" in our own business dealings but...What does this entail? What needs to be done to make this a reality?

Here are a couple of clarifying questions for your ethical reflection:

1. Do emotions really have a role in this reflection process? If so, what is that role?

2. Is it important to accept that effective decisions cannot be solely made on the information you have at the

time, you must also search for what you don't know to be more fully "considerate" in your decision making process?

3. What compliance/ethical processes do you have in place to ensure consideration of ALL implications (that are possible at the time)? What is that format/venue? What people are involved in this process? Is it representative of those that the decision will affect?

4. How transparent is the follow up on the decision once it is made? Is the process made known to all who are affected as to how/why the decision was made? If not, why not?

There are, no doubt, more questions that need to be asked and acted upon, and I'm convinced that was the intent of Buddha. The question now, is that your intent to take this "mindfulness" to a deeper level in your organization?

Your Credibility Depends on Keeping Your "Ethics Guard" Up!

A key focus of ongoing education, especially in compliance/ethics, is to learn from the past, glean the key points learned, and use that awareness to forge ahead in a more reflective, targeted and proactive approach.

This is particularly relevant today with whistleblower issues, huge corporate settlements for wrongdoing, and corporate execs going to jail for fraud, embezzlement, etc.

We can never let our guard down when comes to compliance/ethics. Being vigilant, attentive and discerning needs to be our focus. Being proactive is high road behavior, builds loyalty, fosters positive morale, and can have significant impact on decreasing the odds of a costly lawsuit.

Ongoing compliance/ethics training needs to be non-negotiable, consistently providing techniques, insights, and creative proactive approaches to help all handle any future "questionable" situations. The ways to deliver this training and processes to do follow up, are crucial to keep this point from becoming a "one shot" compliance/ethics training effort. This keeps everyone involved, proactive and engaged. It also ensures everyone sees the value, relevance and importance of keeping their guard up, as well, as how to deal with certain issues when they arise.

Transparency then, becomes the lynchpin to developing a trust dimension, not only among ourselves, but with our customers, and communities. Therefore, one needs to examine how transparent are the decision making processes, policies and procedures? How transparent are the organization's governance structures? For all of these issues create credibility, loyalty and a great "checks and balances" environment for employees, vendors, suppliers, customers, etc.

Equally important in all of this is if one expects this type of commitment and approach to compliance/ethics, is the need to recognize and reward those who have "embraced" this behavior. If employees have shown through their attitude and behavior, the value of being proactively compliant, and ethical, and have been recognized for this behavior by their peers, it's not good only for the individual, but for the company and community at large.

So where is your organization in this process? Are you actively seeking out and rewarding those who demonstrate ethical and compliant behavior, while eliminating, retraining or sanctioning those who don't?

Ethics in Conflict: What Will You Do?

An ethical dilemma is a conflict situation in which what's "right" isn't always clear cut or obvious. Here's a process to consider in resolving an ethical dilemma.

- The leader attempts to clarify any ambiguous facts in or around the dilemma.

- The leader encourages a broad reaction to the dilemma by asking open-ended questions like: "The issue, (not the behavior), here is…" "A solution would need to consider…"

- The leader helps those involved understand, and clarify the positions taken by each individual.

  When you handle the issue this way then you are no longer dilemma-oriented, but are using a process in which each person can respectfully challenge another's thinking/reasoning.

- Through probes and analogies, the leader attempts to place particular opinions that are in conflict into perspective, thus the group moves to a greater understanding of the dilemma and the ethical concepts it contains.

The process certainly involves certain soft skills such as listening, redirecting emotional energy, creating an environment of trust and honest dialogue by setting guidelines like:

- Everybody speaks their "truth". It may not be" THE truth" but it's their truth and needs to be respected.

- Perceptions determine attitudes and attitudes determine behavior. Perceptions are neither right nor wrong. They just are.

- The leader is the facilitator, a catalyst by which there is no judgment only analysis to allow the group to come to ethical consensus and solution.

- The purpose is collaboration and a process that can foster collaboration creating a non-threatening environment of valuing the opinions, insights and wisdom of those involved in the process.

Five Leadership Virtues that Can Make the Real Difference!

People may be born with a tendency to be a great leader, but until they're taught or develop the characteristics of a leader they won't capitalize on that innate tendency. What qualities do great leaders possess? Here are a few:

Trustworthiness

What is your word worth? Do you keep your promises? Remember, trust is the glue that holds any relationship together. It is something that is only earned over time and can't be demanded from others just because you want it.

Unity

Is everyone "on the same page" with goals, initiatives, etc.? Working on the same page, in the same book, for the right reasons are all crucial for keeping everyone focused and pointed in the same direction. How do you model/communicate unity?

Respect

Every human being deserves respect. This is the bottom line. Learn to disagree with behavior but affirm personhood. This is an important differentiation that requires different skills.

To always affirm personhood will always get a leader what one wants from their people.

Justice

What's fair, what's just? According to whom or what? These are key questions to discern. Is it a compliance issue, or an ethics issue? Is it because you think someone is wrong or unethical? You need to identify on what basis justice is meted out and why. Being able to clearly state your reasons and present a clearly reasoned argument is much more effective than saying, "I just think it's wrong," or "I feel like it's wrong." Be specific.

Service and Humility

Humility means to know what your strengths and weaknesses are and to be at peace with that reality. It also means to realize and acknowledge that a leader did not get where he/she is in life on their own. They stand on the shoulders of those who have gone before one. The key question here as a leader is, are your shoulders strong enough for the next generation? This is true leadership based on service to others. Remember, people will only change when they trust the one who created the change.

How to Ethically Balance One's Life.

In order to live a more moral and ethically balanced life I reflect on what author Richard Rohr calls "The Five Facts of Life." Acknowledging these helped me to better prioritize and experience less stress, and more focus. These facts help me be more reflective and appreciative of life. In that spirit I offer them to you. And they are:

Life is difficult...

and once I accepted that fact, life seemed to get less difficult. When I attended a commencement speech a few years ago the speaker made quite an impression on me with the statement *"life is a bumpy road with the occasional smooth spots along the way, not the other way around."* Many of us seem to go through our days expecting life to not only be easy, but to mostly remain that way. When the "bumps" come our response is often to get upset, angry or super-stressed. The simple act of viewing life as a bumpy road (while reminding myself that it is probably one that I can navigate capably) helps me to respond with equanimity when troubles arise.

You are not that important...

in the grand scheme of things we really are not *that* important. There have been millions and millions of people who lived before us and only a small number made their way into the history books. While babysitting my two-year-old grandson, one day I found myself pondering my own mortality and wondering "Who will remember me after him?" Then I thought, "Who cares, just as long as he remembers me!" A sense of our place in the universe, living an honorable life, and doing a good job with the gifts we have been given seems a worthy pursuit — even if we might not be destined to make the impact of a Mozart, Thomas Edison or Nelson Mandela.

You are not in control...

and yet many of us spend a lot of effort trying to be in control. How much of our lives can we actually control anyway? Can we control the weather, the traffic or what happens tomorrow? Have you ever had the experience of everything going nicely and according to plan only to have some person or unexpected event come along to "mess things up"? I prefer to view each day as an opportunity for influence (preferably positive) rather than an opportunity for a wrestling match with control.

You life is not just about you...

and with a little humility we can see that none of us achieved our successes in life totally on our own. Parents, teachers, coaches, mentors — someone else helped us along the way. In that sense we stand on the shoulders of others. So a fair question is: Are your shoulders strong enough for the next generation? Who will you mentor? Who will you encourage? What can you do?

And the last fact is the biggie... *You are going to die...* We try not to think about it, but it is a fact...

In some of my programs I offer what I call the greatest time management principal of them all. It is this: Live each day as though it is your last day and some day you'll actually be right! This line usually gives way first to audience surprise, then laughter — but it is an easy way to help us keep our priorities clear! Did you enjoy the sunrise this morning? Have you told those important to you how much they mean to you? Is there a kind word or deed you can offer today? Why wait?

Is There a Way to "Gauge" One's Moral Leadership?

Socrates and Plato both taught that knowledge and virtue are one in these ways:

- If one knows what is right, then one will do what is right.
- Virtue is a kind of knowledge in that they are deeply ingrained habits that guide one's action.
- The goal of the moral life is to cultivate the very best character one can.

If we use the above as a "gauge" for leadership today, what would this tell us? I would suggest, that by and large, leaders don't examine their lives deeply enough to see the moral dimension of their actions or their decisions. Too much other stuff gets in the way, be it, CYA for your job, placating shareholders, wanting to be re-elected, etc. Morals that are not on one's radar, or the belief that morals have nothing to do with business are dangerous territories to walk. People can see the effect of a lack of moral leadership, often long before you're aware they've seen it.

Do leaders really know what is right? According to whom? For what reason? And for what result? Leaders need to take time to discern their own morals and how they bring them to the workplace and why.

What are the leaders' deeply ingrained habits? How ingrained? Positive or negative? The only way to judge is to observe the leader's actions and their effect on the people around them. These habits need to become "second nature" so that the leader doesn't even have to think about them. Ethical reactions, or doing what is right because it's right, should be an automatic and integral part of one's decision making.

If the goal of the moral life is to cultivate character, what are the keys to character development? It seems to me that character is built on three concepts:

- **Who you are:** the virtues you have acquired over a lifetime, especially virtues like honesty and integrity.

- **What you represent:** your ability to recognize moral issues and choose the "good" without struggling and justification

- **How you act when no one is watching:** the degree of moral internalization you engage in.

So take some time to take a step back, reflect on these questions/points and gauge for yourself how you're doing and what you need to do next.

Trust Is Everything, for Without It You Have Nothing!

"The scholar does not consider gold and jade to be precious treasures, but loyalty and good faith."

~ CONFUCIUS

Is it just me, or is trust "taking a hit" lately? How about politics? Do you feel totally confident about the accuracy of information circulated by political candidates? What about consumer products? Do you ever question the safety or effectiveness of a product, even if backed by a big name brand? How about your healthcare provider? Ever question a diagnosis or treatment plan?

No matter which way you answer the questions above, the element of trust, specifically your determination of trustworthiness, factored into your answer. I view trust as the glue that holds relationships together and serves as the basis for growth, personal or business — as long as trust is present, the relationship is positioned for growth. Once trust is injured or destroyed, restoration of trust can be an uphill climb.

Since it is much easier to maintain trust than to restore it, it's critical that you ensure you have a process or system for re-enforcing that trust. How?

If you are in a position of leadership keep this simple phrase in mind: "morale filters down, not up." Generally, those in leadership positions set the tone. While your position gives you authority over others, it's your behavior that will be pivotal in gaining and keeping people's respect. A disconnect between what you profess and how you behave will cost you credibility and weaken trust.

In the corporate environment, an example of this disconnect might be when "belt tightening" is being required of the rank and file, while at the same time executive bonuses are being reported in the media as the highest in the industry.

Pay attention to your Moral Compass! Just like the benefit of paying attention to your physical health, maintaining an awareness of what is going on around you as relates to your own sense of right and wrong, can be a wise idea. Practicing awareness with regard to moral obligations at home and in the workplace will help if red flags start to make an appearance.

Recognize that trust requires a commitment to "High Road" behavior, and high road behavior includes not only the letter of the law but also the commitment to "doing what is right."

Reputation counts ... You are going to have some kind of a reputation; why not work at making it a great one!

Talk about trust today is not in short supply, but when it comes to actually being someone people trust, or being a trustworthy organization, the field narrows. Actions, not words, become the real test. I think this might be what Alfred Adler had in mind when he offered...

> **"**Trust only movement. Life happens at the level of events, not words. Trust movement.**"**

Leaders Have Got Business Relationships Wrong and it Shows!

In Tom Morris' book, *If Aristotle Ran General Motors*, there was a profound quote about business. Morris wrote: "Business is a partnership of people creating, in many ways, a better life for others as well as ourselves."

The key word in this definition for my business, and I dare say yours, is the word *partnership*. Partnership, in this definition, is based on the question: What can I do for you to get you to cooperate with me? Weren't we all raised with statements like: What goes around comes around; you reap what you sow.

What a different business environment it would be if everyone embraced Tom Morris's definition of business, instead of the corporate mantra of "what's in it for me?"

Partnerships i.e. relationships, are based on trust, other-centeredness, honesty and ethics. In the end, helping others get what they need helps you get what you need. How did this simple truth get so lost in the world today? How did we "lose our way?"

Partnerships are about serving, and about thinking of others before yourself. Partnership is about reaping the benefits that one gets from doing this genuinely and consistently. Isn't this how a business builds a loyal customer base? Isn't this being "value-based and principle driven?"

It is very clear what happens when leaders don't act this way, i.e. read the news and watch the media. You get what you asked for. The challenging question for all is, what are you, as a leader, going to do about it in your business or industry?

Leaders with a Sense of a Moral Compass ...

If leaders don't have a developed moral compass, nothing else they do or produce really counts. Everything about a business needs to be based on values which provide a "direction" as to not only how one does business, but why! Here's why leaders need to embrace as the basis of their moral compass:

1. Because everything happens for a reason and it serves them. There are an infinite number of ways to react to any situation and being values-based needs to be the priority for discerning the appropriate decision.

2. Whatever happens, take responsibility for it, and be accountable. Taking responsibility is one of the best measures of a leader's power and maturity. By being accountable, the leader retains the power to change the result he/she produces and influence other to follow.

3. People are your greatest resource. There is no long lasting success without the right rapport among employees. Leaders who produce results, have a tremendous sense of respect and appreciation for people because those same people have been involved in the results process. Organizations that succeed have leaders that treat people with respect and dignity and see their employees as partners.

So how do you get leaders to "buy into" these concepts? You don't! Either they believe and embrace them or they don't.

The next question is: What type of "screening" is needed to make sure that a potential leader has developed a strong moral compass that emanates from within, and isn't just a show to get past the human resources department?

These three simple points, if actually acted upon, can provide the "destination" that one's moral compass can "set sail" towards that will build an environment of trust, honesty, transparency, and respect for all.

The Non-Negotiable Moral Obligations of Leaders

It's been said of business, "Everything is negotiable," but that's not true when it comes to the moral obligations a true leader takes on.

A. Always put people first in decision making. In a research white paper that I recently read, it said that 57% of all companies that have downsized in the last few years still have the same problems, which tells me that it wasn't the people, but the people were the ones made to pay for the problem of the organization. Maybe it was the process, maybe it was the leaders, maybe it was, whatever, but people need to be considered first in decision making, particularly in the long term. No matter where I have traveled in this country, no matter what organization or business that I've spoken to, they all tell me that, "People are our most important assets." Then why aren't they a priority in many areas of decision making?

B. Respect the individual human dignity — you have a right as a leader to disagree with my behavior, you do not have the right to challenge my human dignity or my self-esteem. There is a difference between telling someone, "You are the dumbest thing next to the jackass," as opposed to, "Normally you don't make decisions this poorly. I was wondering why this decision was made and how you came to that?" Always, always, always affirm personhood; disagree with behavior.

C. Treat everybody fairly. Do the company rules apply for the CEO and all the way down to the new hire? The last thing you need as a leader is a chink in that armor — that there are different rules for management or leadership than there are for the employees. Everybody must play by the same rules. One of the points that I make in my programs is dealing with the codes of ethics. Here's my analogy. If you invite me to your house to play a game, shouldn't you explain the rules before we play? And what happens if you change the rules in the middle of the game?

What happens to your credibility and the credibility of the game? That's what a code of ethics needs to do. These are the rules by which we play here at this company. They will not change and they apply to us all, from the janitorial staff to the C-Suite. If you'd like to join us, these are the rules. If you don't like them and can't abide by them, then maybe you need to find a job someplace else. That's the goal. But within the context of that code of ethics, which reflects the company's mission statement, is the key point that everybody must play by the same rules — everybody. There are no exceptions and no "get-out-of-jail-free-passes" for bad behavior or breaking the rules.

D. Be honest. If you have a short memory, always tell the truth. Every now and then in an audience someone will come up to me and say, "Well you know, I only told a little white lie." Compared to what? A big chartreuse one? How does this work? If honesty is a moral principle, then don't chip away at it. Be honest. Yet how many of these obligations do we see in today's workplace? These obligations are innate capabilities that leaders need to address, communicate and model in their organizations daily! When you do these things, then peace and trust will abide.

Peace, Peace, Where Art Thou?

I think about this question on a regular basis. What does it really mean? When we think about peace, read about peace and even sing about peace, what does that look like?

For many, the focal point of peace is the attainment of peace of mind. Peace of mind seems to be attained when one's values are in alignment with one's behavior. It means knowing what one's values are, what one's "line in the sand" is and behaving consistently on that basis.

Peace of mind can come from something someone said or did. Or it might come from what you said or did. When this happens, you sleep "peacefully." When it doesn't happen, you may keep waking up thinking about that situation. When you have a conscience, you will be painfully aware when your values are not in harmony with your actions. Gauge for yourself how many "peaceful" nights you have vs. restless, sleeplessness nights you have.

Peace of mind can be a needed reflection. *Peace on earth begins with me*, as the song says. How much at peace are you really with your life, family, significant others, the workplace, etc.? As I get older, I really believe that the ultimate goal of life is to be "at peace," as everything else seems to be fleeting.

I wish you Peace and All Good!

Questions to Help Define Ethical Issues and Appropriate Leader Behaviors

Following is a checklist of questions you can use to help you define ethical issues and the commensurate, appropriate leader behaviors:

1. What are specific ethical behaviors that are required of all leaders?

2. What are the consequences if they don't behave ethically?

3. What are the situations that people encounter that could lead them into a grey area?

4. How should grey areas be handled?

5. How should people make decisions when they encounter difficult situations?

6. Where might leaders fall into grey areas while implementing our goals and values?

7. What are the areas where we will not tolerate compromise?

8. What are the areas of flexibility?

9. Where do we need to clarify our mission and values, to make it clear that we are an ethical organization, and ethics are not negotiable?

10. How can we more effectively recruit, recognize and retain ethical leaders?

Reputation: Is the One You Have the One You Want?

I recently overheard a conversation between two people and it went like something like this...

"Did you see that magazine article on 'John Doe'? Didn't you work for him a while back? It was a great article, nice write up, good photos, very positive description of how he grew the business!" The response from the other person was surprisingly lukewarm. "Too bad he was not a very nice guy." I wonder how "John Doe" perceived his reputation: based on the article or on his workplace relationships?

One of my favorite business books is *Values, Prosperity, and the Talmud – Business Lessons from the Ancient Rabbis*, by Rabbi Larry Kahaner. In a concluding section of the book, it states, "the Talmudic rabbis would sum up the secret of business success in one word: Reputation!"

We all have a reputation, but do we spend much time actively thinking about it? It might be productive once in a while to consider if the reputation we want is actually in line with the reputation we have. To help provide introspection, here are a few questions to get the process started:

1. What do you want to be known for in your work? Maybe it is great customer service or being a subject matter expert, your quick response time, being principle driven and ethical.

2. Is there a gap between where you'd like to be and where you are now? Is there a process in place to evaluate how you are doing? As a leader, do you model the behavior that you value? How do others "see" your behavior?

3. Personally, maybe you want to be known as a firm but fair parent or respectful and attentive to your elderly relatives?

4. Maybe you think of yourself as considerate and respectful as a spouse or partner? Do you think you are viewed this way currently? If your answer is no to the last question, then ask if there are any changes you can make to bring the situation into alignment with the reputation you want?

According to the author Ernest Bramah "A reputation for a thousand years may depend on the conduct of a single moment." So...

The Need to Clarify Your Leadership Mission

As business issues and practices can disrupt, challenge and even distort one's mission, time needs to be taken, on a regular basis to stop, and clarify your leadership mission.

Use these questions as a basis to aid the process of self-reflection:

1. What is your basic purpose in your profession?

2. What are (or should be) your principal functions, roles, present and future?

3. What is your uniqueness that you bring to your profession?

4. What is different about your business from what it was 3-5 years ago?

5. What is likely to be different about your business 3-5 years in the future?

6. How will your role/function change and why?

7. What ethical issues, and personal values are important to your future?

8. What do you need to learn or do to meet the challenges of 1-7?

9. Design a plan and timetable to focus on your answer to #8.

If leaders do not continually discern their effectiveness, their mission, and the role ethics and values play in their roles, who isn't shortchanged in the business they're leading?

Tone at the Top: At What Price and Who Pays for It?

Anything that one reads on setting the "tone at the top, had to be disappointed in the stories of the CEO of Walmart knowing about the bribery issues with Mexico, and JP Morgan being ordered to improve their compliance training. Now I find that I'm part of a class action lawsuit of homeowners, against Chase for lowering my home equity amount available based on my home being devalued due to the recession. It has been deemed unlawful.

What a tone at the top! What does this say to employees, customers, vendors, suppliers and competitors? It just seems that no matter how much ethics is stressed, it doesn't seem to be valued to those leaders.

What are the consequences to work for companies in which the senior level leaders "march to a seemingly different drummer?"

Why must the government spend obscene amounts of money to investigate, and prosecute such examples? Shouldn't ethics and ethical leadership be inherent in top leadership?

These types of situations never seem to end and get very tiring. The "bottom line" seems to the motivating factor to "play the odds" of the chance being found out.

Is this kind of stuff legal? I'm not a lawyer so I can't tell you. Is this type of behavior, if proven true, ethical? Absolutely not. A crucial issue, for me, is the same old song of, if it can be proven that one is not guilty, then one acted appropriately.

Really?

Transparency Is the Best Policy and Good Ethics Too!

After much reflection on working with a client on transparency as a focal point of their value statement, I have come to embrace the following insights around transparency, particularly as it relates to ethics:

1. There are people smarter than us out there so don't underestimate them. So, ask yourself, "How much and how long can a person "hide" illegal/unethical business practices before someone "wises up" as to what is going on?" Let's not be stupid here.

2. What about your credibility? Don't people want to do business with people they trust? It's not what you say, but what you do that builds or destroys your credibility.

3. If trust is the basis of all relationships, then what are you doing to develop and keep it? Rather, trust is based on honesty, humility and service.

4. People will follow someone they truly believe in. What do they need to believe in? Truth telling, being other-focused and accountable to all.

5. If there is no sense of pride in an organization, can there be employee loyalty? Pride can either be an evil or a good. Pride in an organization is doing the right thing, at the right time for the right reason and communicating that process to all.

6. Transparency is just good business practice. Transparency is a crucial to an organization's reputation and a good reputation is always good for business.

7. You will sleep better at night if you are *not* dishonest. Being dishonest is extremely stressful in that one needs to remember what one said or did that was not true and isn't there enough stress in life without willfully adding more?

Two Challenging Questions to Keep You Values Based and Customer Focused

How do you evaluate, on an ongoing basis, whether you are on the ethical "right track" in building quality customer relationships that are aligned with your corporate values?

Here are two questions for ongoing ethical reflection:

1. Is what you do, in line with your organization's values and objectives?

2. Will the decision result in right thing being done for the customer?

To further your ethical reflection answer these questions:

Regarding Question 1:

Have you accepted and internalized your company's objectives and values?

- How are the values, that the objectives are based on, communicated?

- How are they reinforced and is it continual?

- Do you truly understand, agree and live those values based objectives?

Regarding Question 2:

- Will the right customer care be delivered no matter the cost?

- Are you truly empowered and encouraged to make the right decision regarding customer relationship building?

- Is this decision sales based or relationship based?

These questions are seemingly simple, yet so much about what you believe, what you've been trained to do and why, need to consistently be the focus of how you do your business.

These questions are continual "reality checks" to make sure that what you profess is what you do.

Being consistently discerning is a win-win situation to keep one's focus, one's values and customer relationships in alignment and that is good for business!

What is the Ethical "Essence" of Work?

When we look at the meaning of work, particularly in today's world, a number of ethical components become crystal clear. The purpose of work is linked to the purpose of education. What is that? The purpose of any education is to find out what you are "good at" and then continue to educate yourself and then use that gift to make the world a better place, because you've been here.

Therefore one must work out of considerations for others, for the society in which we belong and for the whole human family. Isn't the essential purpose of business to offer a service or product for the good of others at a fair price? These three considerations ought to be the essence of why and how we work.

We also need to practice true humility in coming to the reality that we are the heirs to the work of generations who have gone before us and now we share the responsibility in the building of the future of those who will come after us. This is the "ethical essence "of the what and the why we do what we do.

The ethical essence of work lies in the difference between the attitudes of making a living and making a life. Different values for each, not necessarily right or wrong but intrinsically different, with different foci and different results is the basic choice of the meaning of work.

So how's your ethical essence??

What if you had a manager, supervisor or CEO that:

- Took the time to make sure that he/she made the best decision possible at the time, every time.
- Made everyone he/she encountered feel important and worthy of one's time.
- Took the time to associate with people at all levels of the organization.
- Never let issues take precedence in importance over people.
- Internalized discernment as a key part of his/her leadership modus operandi
- Never took credit for the work of others.
- Practiced true humility in his/her management role or position.
- Accepted his/her position but shared the power selflessly.
- Was consistent in how she/he treated each person, regardless of position.

How does this sound? Wouldn't this be a leader to be admired, respected and trustworthy?

If so, maybe we ought to look closely at Pope Francis as an example of leadership skills, including humility, and empowerment. Look closely at how he treats people, acts towards people of all walks of life regardless of religion, politics, etc. Aren't these still admirable qualities that leaders need to strive to attain to be the most effective in their respective roles or positions? I continue to watch and marvel at how this leader really leads!

I am reminded of an example in my own parenting that was truly a "test" of my own character and gave me the insights I listed above. When my son was a freshman in high school, one day he was late coming home, so I periodically would look out the window to see if I could see him walking down the street. Finally I saw him coming, but he was ripping the plastic cover of what looked like a CD and then threw it down the sewer and put the CD in his backpack and proceeded to walk home.

When he got in the house, I asked what it was he tossed down the sewer? He was stunned and gave some ridiculous answer. Then I asked him to empty his backpack and sure enough there was a brand new CD, he had just stolen from Walmart. I, immediately, put him in the car, drove to Walmart, asked to see the manager and explained what had just happened in the last 45 minutes.

The manager took me aside and asked me what I would like to happen. I told him in front of my son, to do with him what you do with anyone who is caught shoplifting. The manager, somewhat stunned of my unwavering support of his position and that a parent would actually take the time to bring a child to justice, lectured my son for a while, and then told him that he was not going to call the police this time, and that my son was banned from the Walmart for the next year.

He told my son that all employees would be notified as to who he is, and what he had done and if my son showed up at the Walmart, the police would be called and charges made.

Needless to say, my son was embarrassed, angry at me for making him go to the Walmart to "fess up" and it put a strain on our relationship for some time to come. But as a parent, the realities of what is right and wrong, goes to the very being of modeling character. If my son had any doubt as to what I stood for, he had no doubt now and that I was more than willing to immediately act on such behavior.

I can only hope that that experience has resonated in his life by the way he behaves and now raises his own son.

Whatever Happened to Honor?

Is the concept of being honorable a thing of the past? Recent situations like fraternity scandals, continual corporate, financial wrongdoings, consistent sectarian dissention in politics, etc., leave people asking who do we trust if anyone? There was a time when a person's word was their bond! I remember my father getting a mortgage on a handshake with a friend who was a banker. If you told someone that you were going to do something, you did it. Trust was the modus operandi and a non-negotiable. How did we learn not to trust?

Even the phrase, "trust me" has taken on a skeptical tone. Being honorable is the essence of reputation, respect, and integrity, and yet, generally, it is not valued or revered. When being honorable becomes obvious, why in the case of a whistleblower is there retaliation and/or punishment?

Honor can't be taught, only modeled. Being honorable does need to be recognized when one recognizes it and sees the value of it. The "consequence" for being honorable is trustworthiness, admiration and a sense of peace. A peace in knowing that one did the right thing for the right reason. When was the last time you were treated honorably? Does that honorable experience outnumber the times when you weren't treated honorably or is it the other way around?

What does your answer tell you about honor?

Why Is the Cost of Being Ethical So High?

I recently received a heart wrenching response to a recent Linkedin ethics post of mine and thought I'd share an excerpt of this response for your ethical reflection.

"I was a whistleblower up against one of the biggest sharks out there. I'm still in the process of writing a book educating people NOT TO BLOW THE WHISTLE. It entirely ruined my life and I lost everything. It is not worth losing your job, your home, your car, etc. I would never again in life speak up in fear of retaliation and go through this all over again."

What would YOU say to this person? What would you do in this situation?

How does ethics make a difference here?

Shouldn't ethical behavior be rewarded and unethical behavior be punished?

What message has this sent to the rest of the employees? This puts into question the theory that doing the right thing, for the right reason, is a good thing.

What a complete waste of ethics training, if there was any at all. This "punishing the whistleblower" solution forces all the employees to develop a "CYA" mentality which affects not only the ethical culture, but workplace morale, customer service, etc.

What is it that these leaders don't get about ethics? Sometimes it takes a poor decision to move leaders to reevaluate their ethics policy. Maybe your organizations could learn from this example, and work to stop this type of reaction that clearly goes against any substantive ethics training.

Would You Hire a Whistleblower?

Would you hire someone who was a whistleblower? If not, what does this say about your organization's ethics program, values, mission statements, etc.? I find that it is easier to intellectually agree with the positions of whistleblowers, i.e. reasons why, cause and effect, etc. but the question would you hire a whistleblower really puts the rubber on the road!

Recent research reports that it takes a whistleblower, on average, three years to find another job! How many jobs were denied due to being a whistleblower I wonder? This type of "punishment" goes against every ethical/moral principle that many organizations preach, train, and communicate to the employees and the public.

Is it that organizations don't want to take a chance that this person would be a hindrance rather than an example of "doing the right thing?"

Conversely, could it not be that hiring this person would send a message that not only do we believe in ethics and ethical behavior but we value the ones who actually "do it?"

Think of the effect of your people for either choice! If your organization doesn't even seriously consider hiring a whistleblower, my experience tells that there are some serious flaws in your ethical culture.

A Code of Ethics Will Not Solve All Your Ethics Problems

According to Aristotle, "... we must remember that good laws, if they are obeyed, do not constitute good government. Hence there are two parts of good government: one is the actual obedience of citizens to the laws, the other part is the goodness of the laws which they obey..." (Aristotle Politics 1294a-6).

Therefore, what are the reasons to have a code of ethics? Research reveals:

1. To help define what are acceptable behaviors.

2. To promote high standards of practice.

3. To provide a benchmark for employees to use for self evaluation.

4. To establish a framework for professional behavior and responsibilities.

5. As a vehicle for company identity.

Given these insights, ask these questions:

- Who decides what's acceptable, the high standards, a benchmark, or a framework? If all of these "come down from on high" can "buy-in" be expected? There must be a venue for all employees to have the opportunity for input for #1.

- Where does the responsibility lie in promoting, reinforcing and enforcing the code of ethics? Compliance, HR, C-suite?

- What has been their training in the process of thinking ethically?

- Is company identity the same as company reputation? If not, what's the difference?

Obviously, much thought and preparation need to go into the development of a code of ethics. So please go slowly. Think critically and implement carefully.

A Code of Ethics Needs to be Differentiated from a Code of Conduct!

A little over a year ago, I was working with a group of senior execs to help them develop a code of ethics for their nationally known company due to a serious compliance lapse. During the facilitation, I used examples of companies that have stellar codes of ethics and over half the execs in the group said: "Why don't we just tweak one of them and call it a day." They just didn't "get it" at this point, but they eventually did "get it."

A code of ethics needs to:

- Be stated positively, i.e. "All employees shall......"
- Refrain from using terms like "right and wrong" as they can be interpreted as very subjective.
- Use terms like: "What's negotiable and what's not?" "What's acceptable and what's not," as the basis for

the development of the code. You're more apt to gain some semblance of consensus than the" right from wrong" attitude.

- Be clear that values/ethics are the basis for the code with the end result as laudable behavior.

- Be understood as company endeavor, i.e. all employees need to have the opportunity to suggest, question, and contribute to the ethics code development.

- Be communicated as a proactive approach as a basis for nurturing desired behavior.

- Include there will be "rewards" for ethical behavior and immediate consequences for unethical behavior.

After facilitating a day and a-half process, this group of execs had created a skeleton of a remarkable code of ethics. We then developed a four month process by which all their employees had the opportunity to help "put flesh" on the code. This collaboration fostered a code that not only gained buy-in from the start but became both acceptable to live by and to embrace.

Now is the time to start the process of either re-vamping your code of ethics or developing one. Remember a code of conduct is compliance based. A code of ethics is ethics based. You need both, so the more proactive you are the better for everyone!!

Can Business Be Ethical and Successful?

Most people will tell you that "business ethics" is a contradiction in terms. "Impossible!" they say. "You have to do everything you can to give customers what they want and increase shareholder value. No one can put ethics before the bottom line and succeed in today's business climate. Ethics just can't be a top priority." And unfortunately, in most cases this view seems to be winning.

What can we do when it seems the bad guys always come out on top? How can we compete in a world where customers ask for incentives that walk a fine line between good service and illegal kickbacks, where unscrupulous salespeople close the deal because they lie, where boardrooms and shareholders alike are screaming for ever-increasing profits while clients demand the lowest possible price, where every bad corporate citizen subjected to a fine knows there are thirty other companies doing the exact same thing?

There *is* a high road to success, one where people live and work according to a set of values, ethics and principles that can make them feel good about themselves and the job they do. More and more companies are learning the power of the high road—they're creating standards for themselves and their employees; they're doing business ethically; and they're acting as good corporate citizens in their communities. As a result, people are proud to work for these companies, customers are proud to buy from them, and shareholders are proud to invest in them.

I believe the high road can actually create *greater* wealth and success in the long term. Material wealth may appear in the form of customer and employee loyalty, community support, and steady, sustained growth. But the less tangible wealth of good will and inner certainty are far more important in the long run. We each have to live with ourselves, and our ethics will determine how good that life is, inside our own heads and hearts as well as inside our companies.

Taking the high road in today's climate of compromise isn't easy. After all, while the low road is paved with easy decisions and immediate payoffs, the high road is full of the potholes of tough decisions and delayed gratification. The high road requires commitment—the willingness to decide what you stand for and how you want your company to be seen. It demands that each of us make choices daily between the easy way and the right way, between getting the sale unethically and not getting the sale at all, between "going with the flow" and standing like a rock against the prevailing tide of ethical compromise.

Ultimately, the benefits of taking the high road are enormous. The high road may not lead you to quick and easy success, but it will enable you to look in the mirror every night and like who you see there. It will allow you to look in the faces of your customers, your boss and your colleagues knowing you have done your best for them, for yourself, and for the greater good. And it will enable you to stand before your children as an example rather than a warning.

Are Compliance and Ethics the Same?

One of the topics that has drawn much response from one of my postings on social media was the confusion about the term; compliance/ethics officer. Compliance is not ethics and ethics is not compliance. They are related but not the same. For example, if you look at practically any compliance/ethics position, it describes legal issues and the position description is usually for someone who is a JD. A compliance officer is, most of the time, an attorney for very practical reasons and rightly so. These are brilliant people in their field. However, your ethics officer is what occupation? Attorney, Philosopher? Theologian? Human Resource Professional? And more importantly what is their formal training in ethics?

Compliance and ethics are like intersecting circles. There is a point where they overlap and both need careful and equal consideration. The question is, when they don't overlap and there is an ethics issue, to whom do your people go for an ethical resolution?

It's important to keep in mind that compliance is a reactive reality, in that one reacts to a law that one did not have anything to do with its creation. Ethics, however, is only proactive. It is a personal choice to be or not. Therefore compliance is letter of the law and ethics is spirit of the law.

Can a compliance ethics officer do both justice? I doubt it! Please don't get me wrong here, I have a tremendous respect for the compliance professionals. They are brilliant people, but ethics is not their formal training. Would you want someone who isn't a JD or trained compliance professional in a compliance position at your organization? Of course not! Well how about ethics? Why would you have someone not trained in ethics, deal with ethics?

It's time to separate the titles and concepts of a compliance/ethics officer or compliance/ethics training (which is it?). Here's another example of what I'm saying. A few weeks ago the county that I live in asked me to consider applying for the role of Ethics Advisor for the County Board. I asked them for a job description and qualifications needed for this position. The job description was all compliance based and the qualifications were either a number of years in county government, a JD,

County board experience, and last on the list, a professor of ethics from a university. I emailed my contact and said that you don't want an Ethics advisor, you want a compliance officer, to which I explained the difference in concept and reality and the reply was maybe I was right!

A client of mine, who is a compliance/ethics officer (and is a JD) in the pharmaceutical industry shared with me his "take" on the difference.

"Simply stated, ethics is the internal intangible that drives us. It's the value system, or lack thereof, that guides us when we make decisions in our day-to-day actions. Compliance is much more clear cut. Compliance is about following the rules, the policies, the regulations that are articulated in laws and internally drafted documents. There are consequences for violating those policies and regulations that can result in discipline up to and including termination. Often, there's no analysis related to intent. If you violate the rules, there will be consequences. Ethics is more about your personal values. I heard an expert say, either you have ethics or you don't. Maybe the rules and regs are for those that don't have guiding principles they live by.

Employees that will do anything to get where they need to go, need a structure in place to stop them from crossing the line. Companies that incorporate a culture of ethical behavior, get employees to follow the rules, not just because they have to, but because it's the right thing to do."

The challenge for companies here is to help their people understand that one can be compliant and yet be unethical. The law is black and white and there are consequences. What do you do when something unethical happens, but it's compliant? What is your process modus operandi? What are the consequences?

In short, compliance, by its very name is a reactive process. To be compliant is to respond to something you have been "taught" to obey, i.e. law. Ethics can only be a proactive process. To be ethical is to focus on values, character, principles, etc what will give you a foundation to make those tough decisions, before they happen.

If companies put as much time, effort and money into ethics training as they do for compliance training, develop proactive, ongoing training in both areas, maybe, just maybe, the way business is conducted, the way people are trained and treated, will take a major step in the ethical direction, which may help people choose to do right, rather than just make them do right.

Now compliance may be more teachable as the law is the law. One must know it, its implications and its applicability in the workplace. This is very important and necessary, however, where does ethics fit into this? Please don't say that ethics is included in compliance training. If it is, ethics probably gets lip service compared to compliance.

Here's another analogy for compliance and ethics. Both are fruit, but one is an apple and one is an orange. Both are good for you, yet they are distinctly different.

"Compliance begins with you."

This is truly a noble theme and yet where is the ethics part?

I would add, "ethics begins with you," as well.

Compliance may be more teachable as the law is the law. One must know it, its implications and its applicability in the work-place. There are so many resources to help with the incorporation of ethics into your everyday training activities. Take some time, look, decide and act.

A starting point for reflection/discussion might be:

1. Can one be compliant and unethical at the same time? If so, how do you handle this?

2. Is your definition of ethics in compliance/legal terminology?

3. Is the perception of your people that compliance and ethics are one and the same?

4. What percentage of the compliance training budget is solely for ethics training?

5. How do you evaluate the "success" of a compliance/ ethics programming?

Now is the time to plan purposefully, intently and creatively for your "Compliance begins with you" programming. Please don't wait too much longer!

Does Corporate Purpose Foster Ethical Leadership?

Corporate purpose is the reason that a company exists and it reflects the intersection of one's corporate mission, goals and values.

But when profit is viewed and embraced as the sole purpose of the company, is then it distorts and corrupts the whole process. However a corporate purpose built on quality relationships based on trust with customers, employees, etc., truly inspires the highest levels of ethical leadership.

Ethical leadership has five key principles that focus on purpose:

1. An ethical leader engages people in a meaningful shared purpose, dialogue and process.

2. The purpose needs to be and should be ethically elevating, in that it raises not only the moral awareness of what a corporation believes, but what it expects, models and reinforces for employees ethical behavior.

3. The ethical leader is successful in creating multi-faceted, consistent, ethics training options in order to elevate the corporation's common purpose for and with all employees.

4. The corporate conscience develops when there is complete and universal "buy-in" to the corporate purpose and how it is going to be communicated, internalized and modeled consistently.

5. If a situation arises when someone reports that someone, process or behavior is not living up to the accepted corporate purpose, then this person should be rewarded somehow by the ethical leaders for having lived out the purpose, mission and values.

Degrees Don't Guarantee Knowledge!

Think about this. In all of your own academic accomplishments, no matter how many degrees you have, did you have many more mediocre/worst teachers or many more best teachers? My research shows that most of us had more mediocre or worst teachers than best teachers. Best teachers are like eagles, in that they never fly in flocks, but only solo. If your best teachers were far and few between, then the majority of your teachers were mediocre at best and sometimes the worst. What a missed opportunity for those who "missed" being a best teacher and what a missed growth opportunity for their students!

Why the disparity? Didn't they all have degrees? What was it about their education that could have made such a big difference in how they relate what they learned? After all aren't we all "teachers" regardless what our position or occupation?

What does "being educated" really mean? Does it only to transfer knowledge or the development of wisdom? Which one was the focus of your best teacher, worst teacher?

Knowledge is the "stuff." Wisdom is what you do with it! Mediocre/worst teachers only gave knowledge and we forgot most of what they taught. Best teachers strove to share wisdom.

Knowledge is only the basis for thought and without the development of wisdom from that, it all falls flat!

Don't Be Afraid of Conscience

In reflecting on current business/political issues, where is the concept conscience evidenced?

Can an organization even have a "conscience?"

Thomas Aquinas defined conscience as "the act of determining that which I ought to do or not do or that one was right or wrong in performing that action." This makes conscience practical.

Isn't this what a code of ethics, a mission statement, or a vision or value statement is supposed to discern for organizations? If so, then why not use the term conscience?

The term conscience is not just something personal any more than the term ethics is just personal. Conscience is also communal, as is ethics.

Could it be that conscience is not well enough understood, accepted or considered relevant to include it in training?

Aquinas goes on to say that: "to disobey conscience is deliberately to choose what is recognized as wrong and to obey conscience is to choose what is recognized as right."

Therefore conscience is always binding! It is binding under the conditions that conscience needs to be well informed and objectively educated. On an organization side then, whose job is it to be proactive in helping one's people internalize the importance of being well informed and objectively educated?

If this is done properly, proactively and with proper intent, then can a person be blamed for obeying conscience?

Excellence, Accountability and Leadership

Periodically I teach a college class on ethics that meets one day a week. With my original roots in education, I am having a great time being back in the classroom, if only on a limited basis...

That is probably why the buzz surrounding the new book *Academically Adrift: Limited Learning on College Campuses* by Richard Arum of New York University and Josipa Roksa at the University of Virginia caught my attention, especially since it happened to coincide with the start of another semester. As described in the New York Times article, "How Much

Do College Students Learn, and Study?" By Jaques Steinberg, (www.nytimes.com)—

> "In the book, and in an accompanying study, the authors followed more than 2,300 undergraduates at two dozen universities, and concluded that 45% 'demonstrated no significant gains in critical thinking, analytical reasoning, and written communications during the first two years of college'."

No significant gains....that can't be good.

When I read the article, a few things came to mind. The first — if I were paying college tuition "no significant gains" would not be a comforting thought! And then I remembered a comment that was made when I was briefed before the start of the first college class I was preparing to teach over a year ago. "They really won't read much." Which, correctly or incorrectly I took to mean—so don't assign them much reading; they won't do it.

There might be something to that comment because also in the above mentioned article was this quote from the book. "...they found that 32 percent of the students whom they followed did not, in a typical semester, take 'any courses with more than 40 pages of reading per week' and that 50 percent 'did not take a single course in which they wrote more than 20 pages over the course of the semester.' "

In fact the students in my first class last year did read and they did write. It took a while for a few of them to realize that reading was an important part of a class on ethics. The wealth of information available and the theory and history of ethics requires a fair amount of reading just to gain a passing acquaintance with the subject. And then there was that business sense of mine which would not allow me to deliver to them anything less than the full value for their tuition dollars.

Not one student (in anonymous exit evaluations submitted after grades were already recorded) made a comment that the material was too difficult or the reading too demanding.

In the role of teacher, I am finding that the questions about what I demand of myself and my students are very similar to the questions we ask in business: Is there moral obligation to deliver an honest day's work for an honest day's pay? Am I delivering to the customer/student the full value for what they were charged for their product, their service or their class?

Are accountability and excellence less important for students and instructors in education today than for businesses or other sectors today?

I think that the following questions are fair questions, no matter if we are talking about business, industry, healthcare, education or government:

- Do I demand excellence of myself? Do I think excellence is a realistic expectation for others?

- Is there a moral obligation associated with my work?

- As a leader do I have an obligation to do my best to create an environment where each person feels included and empowered?

- Does my behavior convey that I place importance on accountability and responsibility?

Excellence—you know it when you see it!

Every Spring parents and grandparents are treated to the annual ritual of the primary school music program. With two granddaughters in public grade school in another state, my wife volunteered, this past spring, to make a midweek trip to attend their program. She is a music lover, and encouraged our own kids (trumpet, piano, and viola lessons) and now the grandkids, to value music and music education.

She noted that there was a particularly beautiful choral piece performed by the 5th grade choir. The choir director provided a little background on the music, the composer and then mentioned to the audience that it was a "very difficult piece." At the conclusion of the selection the room was initially quiet, she related "and then the wave of a standing ovation overtook the gym turned concert hall." The "difficult" piece had been performed flawlessly!

I could not help but reflect when my wife and I discussed the concert after she returned home, that at the heart of this was one music teacher, a leader who clearly believed in excellence, believed that she was accountable to herself and her students to offer her best, and believed that together she and her students were capable of mastering that "very difficult piece" and so much more.

Finally, realize the insights of this Greek proverb...."What is good to know is difficult to learn."

How Is Thinking Ethically Different from Thinking Legally?

Making a proper ethical decision is challenging. Why is that? The process of thinking ethically is uniquely different from thinking legally. Therefore, here's a format to help in that process of thinking ethically to compliment and challenge your compliance training.

1. What should we do?

One needs to reflect on not what one can do but what should one do. We need to get beyond what can be done, which normally is the case, to should we do this, focusing the decision being values-based and principle-driven. Your "should" should be reflective of and find its basis in the ethics training and focus.

2. What do we know?

What we need to consider is not just what we know, but find out what we don't know because what you don't know can drastically affect the decision making process.To make a decision on the basis of only what we know at the time, is to rationalize the decision. Ethics is not about rationalizing but working to be objective.

3. What does it mean?

We need to get the real meaning, focus or value of the essence of why we want to do a certain action. Unless we understand the "meaning", that gives us a better basis for our decision, the decision may just be a Band Aid on an artery problem.

4. Why does it mean that?

We need to get the source of the meaning. Is it the values of how one was raised or trained? Is it from life experience? The reason for meaning will give direction and focus to a more substantive and ethical decision.

Use these questions to help formulate, challenge and integrate into your ethics training for your Fall programs, conferences or meetings and see what happens!

Fraud and Ethics Never the Twain Shall Meet!

In one Frontline documentary on PBS called "Untouchables," the program pointed out that no CEO banker who was involved in the mortgage crisis was ever charged, prosecuted, or jailed! Not one! Additionally, a number of congressmen tried to move the process along, but to no avail.

How can this be? While England sent a number of bankers to jail, the U.S. seemed to have looked the other way. I bet banks like Citibank, JP Morgan Chase, etc. have an ethics training program. But what good does an ethics program, no matter how good it is, do if the CEOs and Senior Executives of these banks are not ethical? Not that they would admit it, but customers can see what is happening. Does anyone really believe that compliance and ethics are the same thing? If they do, it's more for convenience for their agendas than it is a reality.

What this program pointed out was that nothing could be proven legally, and no one knew where the buck stopped. Some CEOs were brought before Senate hearings, House hearings and grilled about their involvement in this scandal. Still, not one was charged, arrested or prosecuted.

Never mind the legal issues for those guilty of the actions were serious enough, but what they did was unethical! Millions of people have/are suffering because of the greed at any price attitude. The CEO of Countryside had a license plate that said "FUNDIT". No matter the credit score, or if one had a job, give everyone a mortgage! How moral is this?

If morale filters down and not up...?

Where is the accountability for these actions?

The sad thing is that people have become increasingly lethargic regarding issues like this. The apathy is great, it's almost permission giving!

Watching this program was informative, frustrating, and called into question, "Where was the ethics in all of this?

How Can You Improve Your Ethics Training?

Here's a checklist to help you evaluate how your ethics training is going so far this year to help you plan your ethics training for the next year.

Consider these 10 questions as part of your annual ethics training evaluation:

1. Is there ethics training for employees on all levels?

2. How is the process of thinking ethically being implemented?

3. How does your organization consistently communicate its commitment to ethics to its employees?

4. What are your evaluation standards to discern your ethics training effectiveness?

5. Are the differences and likenesses between compliance training and ethics training clearly delineated and understood?

6. Is the approach to ethics training one of continual analysis, updating, and pertinent to the workplace?

7. Are employees encouraged to question authority when asked to do something they consider wrong?

8. Is your ethics hotline really working? Is it an internal hotline or a contracted out hotline?

9. How is unethical behavior dealt with? Immediate? If not, why not?

10. How is ethical behavior rewarded? If not, why not?

As you ponder your answers to these and other questions that may arise, what are your ethics training opportunities that you should be thinking about implementing? Isn't now the time to do so?

How Do You View Your Ethical Culture as a Business Advantage?

Reflective questions as per your role and position.

1. How would you define an ethical culture?

2. What makes your culture ethical?

3. Since you see this as a business advantage, how would you each evaluate how it is an advantage?

4. How do you continually sustain this culture?

5. How do you see this culture communicated to your employees/vendors or suppliers?

6. How do you plan to keep your culture current, relevant and substantive?

Develop A Moral Compass

"Your moral compass can only point you in the
right direction. It can't make you go there."

~ ANONYMOUS

Our moral compass is that internal ability to determine what is
right or wrong and to determine what actions we should take
based on that awareness. It is not the discipline or strength
to act on that knowledge. That comes from a long history of
practice doing the right things.

How Does One Set a Moral Compass?

Let's fall back for a minute to the basics of compasses in general. If you've never used a compass to find your way in the wil-
derness, the first thing you need to know is that the needle on
a compass always points to magnetic north — unless it comes

too close to something that disturbs the needle, causing it to give a false reading of where north actually lies.

Even when you've determined "true north" and have eliminated all distracting or disturbing objects that can give you a false reading, you must still check the compass every few hundred feet to make sure you haven't stumbled upon something else to skew the needle's direction. Compasses, whether actual ones, or moral compasses, need to be consistently calibrated to ensure we aren't being led astray.

Where are the "moral compasses" today? Congress? Education? Business? Sports? And if one finds an organization or person with a moral compass, what does it look like and how does it work? Is there evidence that the compass is being regularly calibrated? Are the people and challenges that would disturb the needle's ability to point to "true north" being eliminated or neutralized? Are people with a broken moral compass being fired or retrained?

The purpose of a compass is to set a direction and help discern a course of action on how to get where one wants to go. The compass is the tool, but sometimes people and organizations need to learn how and why to use their moral compass properly. They need to be aware that circumstances, people, decisions, outcomes and consequences can alter the accuracy of their compass, or cause it to confuse a true reading.

With a moral compass, the added dimension of morals, or "true north" comes into focus. The premise for using this compass properly is that one knows what one's values and morals are and that, in an ideal world, knows one's "line in the sand" that will not be crossed.

Isn't one's "line in the sand" the goal of a moral compass and the modus operandi of a moral compass. What is the "true north" for a moral compass? Is it the law? Is it the common good?

Unless one knows what "true north" is morally, can one really have a moral compass?

The moral compass is not just what one believes or states it is, it must pervade every decision made, big or small for consistency sake. Without that consistency, can there be a viable moral compass? In a perfect world we could set a literal compass and follow it unerringly. But as in the physical and business world, compasses must be constantly recalibrated.

Given these trying times in politics, international relations, religious institutions, professional sports, to name a few, is having a viable moral compass even possible, and can employees and leaders be counted on to ensure that it is consistently checked, calibrated and accurate?

How Would You Know if Your Leaders Are Ethical?

Now is the time to step back and take a good hard look your ethical leadership development and examine what needs to be done differently, creatively and substantively before another quarter gets away from us?

The test of the true ethical leader may lie in the answers to these questions:

1. **What are specific ethical behaviors that are required of all leaders?** Who or what established this list and why? How are they communicated? Consistently?

2. **What are the "prices to pay" if they don't behave ethically?** Are the consequences in direct proportion to the behavior? How immediate is the consequence? Does this apply to everybody, i.e. Board of Directors, Senior Execs, etc.?

3. **What are the situations that people encounter that could lead them into grey areas?** Ethics can

only be proactive. Once identified, how proactive is your ethics training to prepare for these "grey areas?"

4. **How should grey areas be handled?** What techniques, tools, resources are provided to help make the proper moral decision?

5. **How should people make decisions when they encounter difficult situations?** Based on what? What's best for all concerned, amount of profit, what one can get away with or ??

6. **What are the areas where leaders will not tolerate compromising values?** Do they know what's acceptable/what's not acceptable? What's negotiable/what's not negotiable? If not, why not??

7. **Where do we need to clarify our mission and values, to make it clear that we are an ethical organization, and ethics are not negotiable?** Are your mission/values statements dated, i.e. over 3 years old? Is your code of ethics stated positively or negatively?

8. **How can we more effectively recruit, recognize and retain ethical leaders?** Are a person's values considered in the hiring process and performance reviews? How consistent, integral and

relevant is your values based leadership development program?

If you have a problem answering any of these questions, maybe they should be topics for a more in depth values based leadership development program?

SECTION FOUR
Practice Accountable Leadership

"Accountability breeds responsibility."

~ STEVEN COVEY

You can be accountable without being responsible, but if you are, you won't last long. Leaders must be both accountable and responsible, and willing to own both their failures and successes. True leaders will recognize that unless those they lead or supervise are also accountable and responsible, they can't have a quality organization, team or company.

In the following section I share a variety of insights I've gleaned over the past two decades.

If Ethics Is Not a Priority, Why Should Someone Work for You?

I regularly suggest to job seekers that one of the first things to ask a prospective employer is what is their code of ethics? If they can't produce one, think twice about any possible job offer. Why? Because if a company can't tell you what their values are, how they are implemented, how ongoing the ethics training is, what else can't they tell you?

Here's a short series of questions to start the reflection on your company's ethics initiative and where other ethics training opportunities may lie:

1. Do you have a code of ethics? If not, why not? If so, do all employees have a copy of it? Does the company provide ongoing ethics training to reinforce the code? Is the format working?

2. With so many different formats for learning, how do you know which one is the most effective? Is your ethics training a "one shot" deal or is it ongoing?

3. Are all employees, from the top down, required to participate in ethics training?

4. What are the options for your people to confidentially report unethical behavior, i.e. hotline, ombudsman, ethics committee? How well are they utilized? If not,

do you know why? If they are, how expedient and justly are you in dealing with the issue?

5. Do you reward ethical behavior and punish unethical behavior?

6. What type of ethics training do your new hires receive? If none, what does that say?

Invest Now or Pay Later: A Real Ethics Issue

Numerous companies have been fined millions, if not billions of dollars, lost thousands of employees, and have had to deal with negative publicity, and tarnished reputations due to ethics scandals. The results are more than financial, they're personal. Employee lives are also affected, even ruined by association.

So how do you proactively decrease the odds of an ethics violation from happening?

Consider the following questions to take a proactive approach to your ethics training:

1. Do you have a "zero-tolerance" policy? (if not, why not?)

2. Do you have a formal, updated within the last three years, code of ethics? Did all employees have the opportunity to provide input to its creation?

3. Do you provide concentrated ethics training (separate from compliance training) for all employees?

4. Is your ethics training a "one shot" approach or is it continual and consistent?

5. How does your organization communicate its commitment to ethics and ethical behavior to its employees?

6. Are all employees encouraged and empowered to take responsibility for their choices and actions?

7. Are all employees encouraged and supported to question authority when asked to do something they consider wrong?

8. What avenues of communication are available to employees to report unethical behavior? How do you keep this confidential? How do you handle any retaliation?

9. Is misconduct dealt with swiftly, firmly, justly and with transparency in your organization?

10. Does your organization continually emphasize and reinforce to all executive leaders that they must be models of ethical behavior at all times?

Either way, your organization will pay! Be proactive and invest in an ongoing ethics training program or when a violation occurs for lack of ethics training, pay so much more in fines, reputation, etc. Which option will really cost you more? These questions might be a starting point for your program development.

Is There Such a Thing as Situational Ethics?

If there is such a reality as situational ethics, what would be the basis for the decision, the situation or ethics?

Just the term, as I have heard people use it, seems to be used to justify one's actions, therefore making it a subjective approach to ethics. The presumption may lie in the belief that, "the ends justify the means." But do they? And if they do, then explain why and how the ends justify the means? Maybe it's only because someone wants to support or justify his/her decision based upon their moral compass having gone off true north.

Should situations be judged only within their context instead by guiding ethical principles? Which should come first? When one is involved on a particular situation, the temptation, if you will, is to let the situation dictate the interpretation of ethics. If this is the case, I wonder how strong one's ethical/moral compass really is?

The situation is really the test of one's ethics or moral fiber and not the other way around. The situation should not be the deciding factor of one's ethical approach to it, but rather the situation is the challenge of how one applies ethics to the situation without compromising one's ethics. This is what is commonly referred to as applied ethics.

The challenge is, applied ethics need to be an integral part, if not the focus, of ethics training, i.e. in order to maintain one's ethics in a situation rather than let the situation dictate the interpretation of one's ethics.

SECTION FIVE
Stewardship

"Stewardship. It's not just about giving
money, it's about giving everything."
~ ANONYMOUS

Stewardship is an ethic in itself. Stewardship is about the responsible planning and management of resources, be they financial, environmental or human. The concepts and ethics of stewardship can be applied to natural resources, economics, health, property, information, talents, theology, or capital of any kind.

Stewardship isn't just a skill set. It's a way of life, of thinking about things, people and the world around us. Stewards have responsibilities and accountability because they manage the property of others, whether that property is financial or human capital. The questions you need to ask yourself are, "Am I a good steward of what I have been entrusted with?" and, "Am I hiring good stewards to help me do that?"

The Leadership Moral Imperative

We're used to making decisions. But the really tough decisions are those where there's **right and wrong on both sides**, or where our decisions may cause pain to another individual or to ourselves even when we "do the right thing.".

It's important, first, to understand just how we make decisions, and second, to have a method of evaluating things so we can make the tough choices with a clearer mind and easier heart.

So, how are we conditioned to make decisions?

Jean Piaget, a Swiss child psychologist, studied the ways children make decisions, and constructed a theory of what he called the "stages of moral development." Later another psychologist, Lawrence Kohlberg elaborated on Piaget's theory and applied it to adult decision-making as well.

This work states that, as we go through life, our decisions are **based upon different factors**, arranged in a **logical progression**.

Stage 1: Through the Threat of Punishment.

That's how a lot of us were raised growing up: "If you don't clean your room, you can't go to the party." Punishment deals with **fear and external motivation** — not a very high place from which to make a decision, and certainly not a way to run a business or corporation.

Stage 2: Reward

"If you clean your room, I'll buy you that jacket you want." This is how we turn our kids into capitalists. Reward is great motivation, but unless you want to be held hostage by constant demands, it's not effective. If your kids or any of your employees ask you, or imply this attitude of: "If I do that what will you give me?" you know they're motivated only by reward.

Stage 3: The Concept of Good and Bad

You're a good employee if you do this, a bad employee if you do that. However, the terms "good" and "bad" are relative. They mean the person doing the speaking is making a value judgment. If I call my employee "good," what I'm really saying is, "You did what I wanted you to do."

But does that necessarily mean that the employee sees it in the exact same way?

No. He or she could be saying inside, "Boy, that was a stupid way to get that done," or "Gee, that wasn't the kind of service I wanted."

Stage 4: Rules and Regulations

Did you ever hear your parents say, "As long as you live in this house, you'll do the dishes" or "take out the garbage" or some other list of chores? Every business also has rules and regulations for its employees' behavior.

Boss or staff, we all have to live with rules and regulations.

However, what's directing our choices in all of these cases — punishment, reward, good and bad, rules and regulations? It is all based on external forces. We're deciding based upon what other people are telling us, not what we're telling ourselves.

Stage 5: Choice and Commitment.

As you grew up, you began to make more and more choices for yourself, right? You chose the courses you took in school, whether to go to college, what you majored in, where to live, who to date. You chose and then committed to that choice.

Whether it's the kind of peanut butter you buy or the job you take, choice and commitment form the basis of most adult decisions.

Stage 6: Internalization.

You become what your choices are. You are a doctor, or a cop, or a secretary. You're married or single. And the great thing is, you can continue to evolve every minute based upon your choices. None of us are truly stuck in what we are because we're constantly evolving, constantly becoming something different and hopefully better. Becoming is the essence of living—you only stop becoming when they put shovel dirt on your casket.

To be the best person, manager or employee we can be, we need to be operating from the highest possible level of decision-making. That level is where we have internalized the ethics and values that are important to us and where we allow ourselves to evolve as human beings, managers, workers, parents, spouses, and children.

These stages of development are extremely useful when we examine our decisions from an ethical perspective.

The first step to becoming the best you can be is to identify your own level of decision-making skills. This is an important awareness to have, because you cannot lead people beyond where you are right now. The goal is for you and your associates to make decisions based upon choice, commitment, and the internalization of your choices.

You want to choose and commit to the values of your company, and internalize those values so completely that there is no question about the appropriate and ethical response in any situation.

Understanding the Stages

How can you tell where people are on this scale? If someone is working on **Levels One through Four**, they often ask, "What do I have to do?" In contrast, if they're operating on **Levels Five through Six**, they use the phrase, "What can I do?"

Your people's actions as well as their responses will tell you where they are. Learn to look at their actions as well as their words. Some employees will quickly learn what you want to hear. It's harder to face actions than it is words.

It's your job as the leader to empower your people to move to a different stage, to a different level of relating and motivation, but only if you are on the level you want your team to function on.

Therefore the onus is on the leader to be able to discern not only where your people are on these "stages" but more importantly the "stage" you're on, as a leader, because you cannot lead people into a land or challenge you haven't been to, navigated or experienced yourself.

So what level are you on?

Training Time for Senior Leaders and Boards of Directors Is on the Decline

According to a NAVEX GLOBAL recent ethics and compliance study:

> *"While respondents reported that annual training time for non-management employees rose by about 60 minutes from last year (to 7.1 hours) and training times for middle managers stayed about the same (at 6.5 hours), senior leader training times dropped by nearly 90 minutes to 4.4 hours. Board training times also declined by an hour (to 2.0 hours). Losing training time for boards and senior leaders is a disconcerting trend — particularly because without the most senior leaders setting the right "tone at the top," compliance professionals will find it very difficult, if not impossible, to meet their stated top objective of creating a strong culture of ethics and respect."*

So if executive ethics training is not given a priority or the time to provide this, start by answering these questions:

1. What are specific ethical behaviors that are required of all leaders?

2. How is your existing leadership training program incorporating this into their training?

3. What are the consequences if they don't behave ethically?

4. What are the situations that leaders encounter that could lead them into a grey area and how is a "grey area" defined?

5. What is the difference between making an excuse or coming up with a reason for one's behavior, could lack of ethics training be one of them?

6. Leaders need to develop a code of ethics for all that focuses on: what is negotiable and not negotiable and why? What is acceptable and what is not acceptable and why?

7. Does your mission statement make it clear that this is an ethical organization and that ethics are a non-negotiable?

8. What are the obstacles to effectively recruit, recognize and retain ethical leaders?

The above questions will help you in your training initiatives.

"Line-in-the-Sand" Ethics: What Do You Stand For?

The story of the Alamo is a powerful part of Texas history. In 1836, 189 men were holed up in an old adobe church against thousands of seasoned Mexican soldiers under General Santa Anna.

The task of leading the Alamo defenders fell to Colonel William Barrett Travis. It is difficult to imagine the range of emotions that he experienced as a leader....specifically as he came to the awareness that they were alone in the small adobe, church-turned-fort, that help was not coming and that they faced certain defeat and death. The image of Colonel Travis tracing a line in the sand with his sword and asking the defenders to cross the line of they would remain with him to fight to the end, spoke to me about leadership, courage and making difficult choices.

I use this story to illustrate that there are times and circumstances that may require us to "draw a line in the sand" or conversely we may be faced with a situation where we may be asked to "cross a line."

While we may never be asked to respond to a request as serious as the one made by Colonel Travis, it is quite possible that at some point, we may be asked to make a choice that is quite difficult. As much as it would be ideal, we cannot count on always having the luxury of long and careful deliberation on difficult issues. A little advanced thought and planning might help if we are ever in a tight spot down the road and charged with making a difficult choice.

Is there something we can do now about a possible future situation? I think so! Keep alert and periodically evaluate what is going on in your industry, department or workplace. At the same time make sure that you are familiar with your industry's best practices and your organization's code of ethics and conduct.

Consider, before something really serious happens, what would you do if you are asked to do something which goes against your personal code and/or your organization's code of right and wrong. Knowing your "line in the sand" ahead of time and being mindful about where you stand on difficult issues, can help to put good choices, for good reasons, on auto-pilot.

The defenders of the Alamo knew why they were there. Those 189 men crossed that line knowing they would never go home, would see their wives and children again and yet they were still willing to sacrifice themselves for the future of Texas.

What's your line in the sand? Will you be able to hold it as easily as you drew it?

Moral Credibility: The Elusive Leadership Trait

How does one develop moral credibility? How is it manifested on the job? It's like how does one display sincerity? What are the signs of being sincere? Moral credibility needs to reflect the qualities of character, trust, empowerment, positive self-esteem and of course, ethics.

Moral credibility is the sum total of one's consistent behavior in the face of challenging decisions and situations that has as its focus, trust. Moral credibility is modeling and instilling a balanced approach to discernment that is not based on an emotional reaction to a situation.

Yet...how is this credibility learned? Is it life experience? Is it a teachable concept? Is it the result of conditioning? The bottom line is that moral credibility needs to be modeled and observed by everyone in the company. It needs to be modeled with consistency, communicated beyond words, and authoritative in attitude to be truly real.

When one thinks of truly effective leaders, no matter in what industry or field, being credible, sincere and trustworthy are among those critical attributes that separate them from other leaders. Yet, when one reads and/or watches the news or reflects on the environment of one's workplace, it seems that this type of leader is in the minority in today's world.

I wonder why?

Moral Hypocrisy: A Serious Issue?

> "Moral hypocrisy is when one's evaluations of their own moral transgressions differ substantially from their evaluations of the same transgressions committed by others."
>
> ~ ANN TENBRUNSEL AND MAX BAZERMAN

Moral hypocrisy is a case of "don't do as I do, but" do as I say. I love the concept of moral hypocrisy because it is so absurd and outrageous. It's a tremendous way to point out to trainees and readers how far people will go to avoid responsibility or accountability for their actions. And yet horrifyingly enough, it seems so prevalent as to be widely accepted. Why is it that one doesn't recognize this type of attitude? It can't be ignorance. It must be a conscious choice or an unintentional lapse of judgment? Or worse, it's an indicator of a severely broken, or entirely missing, moral compass.

Is moral hypocrisy, or a moral lapse, a case of one's actions preceding a thoughtful consideration, of consequences or is this a premeditated choice?

Underlying all these questions, is a more serious issue. The issue is the attitude of leaders that business is a game and therefore ethics and morality have no significant place or role in the game. It seems that as long that there is significantly more money coming in than there is going out, all can be made well. For example, consider the many billions of dollars that certain prominent banks have made without seeming to care about the millions, or even billions that must be paid out in fines. They accept these fines without anyone seemingly being held accountable for the behaviors that resulted in the fines? It almost appears to outsiders that this is simply how business is done. What if branch managers of these banks caused serious legal issues, would they still work there? Would they not be held accountable? Why not their leaders?

So does this "game" need to be changed or the ones are the ones who are playing it? This is the moral question and dilemma.

People Listen with Their Eyes So, What Are They Hearing?

Leaders need to be clear what is acceptable, what is not acceptable and why in dealing with protocols, attitudes, approaches, and processes. So what are the areas of acceptability?

Where do leaders need to clarify their mission and values, to make it clear that they are an ethical organization, and ethics are not negotiable? How often is your code of ethics reviewed, updated, etc.? Clarifying is integral to being transparent. So what vehicles are used to make transparency a norm?

It is becoming increasingly important that leaders need be more proactive in their approach to the ethical considerations of their roles, power and influence on their people and respective organizations.

Here are few questions to help, at least, start ethical reflections on leadership and to be used as a springboard for more in depth discussions on the ethical roles of leadership.

- **Are the ethical expectations of leaders realistic?** How is this proactively communicated? How often? Is this part of the ongoing leadership development training?

- **What is the price to pay for unethical behavior?** Are these explained prior to any unethical behavior happening, so that one could say that "they didn't know?" Are the consequences administered immediately? If not, why not? How are these situations and consequences communicated to the organization?

- **How are leaders empowering their people with critical thinking skills?** How are you identifying these situations? Who are you asking? Have you identified a proactive approach to create a preventive measure to limit these types of situations from happening?

- **When right and wrong lines are "blurred," what do leaders do?** Who handles this process, i.e. an ethics officer, ombudsman or ethics committee? How is this process communicated to the organization?

- **What skills, techniques, training are leaders using to help their people handle difficult situations?** Are your people trained in ethical decision-making? How is this reinforced? Is there a "process" that has been communicated to be followed when a difficult situation arises? Who or what has the final authority over the decision-making process?

- **Where might leaders fall into grey areas while implementing our goals and values?** Grey areas are the testing ground for one's values. Grey areas are not usually a right vs. wrong scenario, but a right vs. right scenario. So how are the leaders trained to deal with this issue?

- **What are the areas that are non-negotiable?** Leaders need to express what is negotiable, what is not negotiable and why BEFORE something happens.

- **What are leaders doing specifically to hire right the first time, continually provide opportunities for further education in ethics, decision making, teamwork, etc.?** What pre-hiring resources, tools, etc. are there to help "choose right" the first time? When people feel like they belong and receive recognition, you get cooperation, loyalty, trust and retention. So what are you doing to help your people feel like they belong and are recognized for their contributions to your organizations?

Service and Humility: The Keys to Values-Based Leadership

Service and humility are two of the most unappreciated virtues needed for truly effective leadership. Here's what I mean by this. None of us, and I mean, none of us, has gotten where we are in life on our own! Doesn't matter what your title is, what industry you're is in, if the business is a for profit or non-for-profit, small business or a large corporation, all leaders need to recognize this reality.

We all stand on the shoulders of those who have gone before us. All of us!! Whether those shoulders belonged to a parent, teacher, coach, friend, colleague, someone at work, etc., we gleaned insights, knowledge, wisdom, values, morals, self worth, faith etc. and because of that interaction and experience they still, consciously or unconsciously, affect every decision you make.

If you think that you got where you are in life on one's own, you're a fool. If you really believe that you are where you are in life on your own, your ego is way out of whack.

When was the last time you thanked one of those people who had a positive influence on you? How about your best teacher, an involved parent, an insightful coach, a best friend, clergy, etc.? If you haven't yet, please don't waste any more time, thank them now. Being grateful is a key component of service and humility.

Once we come to understand that we stand on shoulders of those who have gone before us, humility follows and in that humility, service to others needs to be the natural outcome.

Here's the real leadership test:

As you recognize and appreciate that you stand on the shoulders of others, are your shoulders strong enough to support those who follow you?

Should an Organization Really Oversee its Own Ethics Reporting System?

Research has shown that the vast majority of companies' ethics hotlines are not utilized effectively due to fear of retaliation. Why is that? What is the process of following up with a compliant? What scares one's people from doing so?

When it comes right down to it, shouldn't organizations want its people to report any ethics/compliances issues? Reporting them would be a reflection of the values that an organization has trained its people to believe in, communicated, and expect values based behavior in the workplace. Why then does a system fail when it comes to actually behaving in accordance with those values?

Can an organization really oversee itself? If organizations REALLY took their values seriously, they would be rewarding those who report violations of the core values on which a company says it's based. In fact, the term "whistleblower" would never be used, because it is degrading. Instead a term like, values advocate, should be used because they are reporting behaviors that challenge the very values and ethics that the organization trained them to embrace and that affect the morale, productivity and the workplace environment . If one's own organization can't see the value of this then something is seriously wrong. Maybe leaders ought to:

- Find another and/or additional options for overseeing the reporting of ethical/compliance violations.

- Find a system that will make all involved in investigating an issue accountable and responsible for the process and resolution.

- Find the proper reward, not punishment, for those who report violations.

- Make sure that anyone who violates the sacred trust of confidentiality, anonymity, and retaliation should be punished, i.e. terminated, suspended, etc.

- Is this really that difficult? Do you believe in your values or not? Is ethics important or not? What lengths should you go to protect those who live those values for the betterment of all?

The Lesser of Two Evils is Always...

Why is it that this phrase is the modus operandi for so many people when making serious and important decisions? Why is it that people settle for the lesser of two evils? Is the lesser of two evils an ethical decision?

It seems that we have been conditioned to choose based on who or what would cause less damage, or evil, knowing and accepting the fact that indeed damage or evil would be done. Why is it that looking for "good" does not seem to be a consideration? Is it too much work? Is it that "good" is not available or is it that it really isn't that important for us personally to be vested in any decision or situation that would cause us to be challenged, particularly if the decision would not affect me directly?

Don't a significant number of voters vote for "the lesser of two evils?" How many times have each of us made a decision on "the lesser of two evils?"

Searching for a "good" option is the ideal, but it takes time, discernment and commitment for personal follow through. Searching for a "good" option is the ethical quest for the values based person. It reflects an attitude that each decision is indeed, important and needs to be made in the context of personal accountability.

Maybe we should be ethically training our people to choose the greater of two goods! I wonder what that would look like?

Are You An Ethical Leader?

Values, Virtues and Leadership

In these challenging times for many businesses, leaders need to periodically take a step back and spend time in reflection as to what their real influence is in their respective workplaces. Take time at the beginning and at the end of each day to ponder on how well you've done in staying true to values, mission, purpose and relationships.

Here's an example of reflective questioning I found in my research.

1. Did I practice any virtues today?

    - Were you a person who shared and modeled integrity, trustworthiness, honesty or compassion?

    - How did people around react to you today?

    - Think of the best teacher you ever had and then make a list of all those characteristics of what made that person the best teacher. Every day before you go to work read the list and decide this is what you want to be remembered for.

2. Were you more positive than negative in your attitude and behavior?

   • Consider the short term vs. long-term consequences of your actions.

   • Did you affirm, in some way, every person you encountered today?

   • Remember, affirm self-esteem and disagree with behavior and work at recognizing this distinction every day.

3. Did I treat people with dignity and respect?

   • All human beings have the right to be treated with dignity simply because they are human.

   • Did you consciously try to separate personhood from behavior in each difficult situation?

4. How did I practice justice today?

   • In what ways did you benefit those around you? In what ways were you a hindrance?

   • On what basis did you decide what was just, i.e. Mission Statement, Code of Ethics, Values statement, the law?

- How did you explain the decision? How was it accepted? What could you have done differently?

5. Did I make my organization better because I was there today?

  - Was I better because I was a part of this organization?

  - Was I able to get beyond my own interests to make the organization stronger?

  - Was I able to draw upon the strengths of the organization to help me become more human?

It is important to remember that people tend to listen with their eyes more than with their ears. What you do, says so much more than what you say.

Consistent role modeling along with ongoing education in behavioral ethics, values and virtues, is a "slam dunk" combination for personal and business success.

Summary:

In a perfect world ethics and moral awareness shouldn't need to be taught, or explained, or put into a book for discussion. But this is not a perfect world. In spite of the allure of "situational" ethics and the ease with which any CEO or manager can blame the company culture or pass the buck, the real question comes down to what kind of man, woman, or leader are you?

And what kind of leader do you want to be? Study after study shows that while the unethical leaders often make fast, short term gains, in the long run the true winners are those companies, cultures and leaders who are consistently loyal, moral and ethical.

What is the Ethical "Essence" of Work?

When we look at the meaning of work, particularly in today's world, a number of ethical components become crystal clear.

The purpose of work is linked to the purpose of education. What is that? The purpose of any education is to find out what you are "good at" and then continue to educate yourself in those areas. When you become skilled in those areas, then you can use those gifts to make the world a better place, because you've been there.

Therefore one must work out of consideration for others, for the society in which we belong and for the whole human family. Isn't the essential purpose of business to offer a service or product for the good of others at a fair price? These considerations ought to be the essence of why and how we work.

We also need to practice true humility in coming to the reality that we are the heirs to the work of generations who have gone before us and now we share the responsibility in the building of the future of those who will come after us. This is the "ethical essence "of the what and the why we do what we do.

The ethical essence of work lies in the difference between the attitudes of making a living and making a life. Different values for each, not necessarily right or wrong but intrinsically different, with different foci and different results is the basic choice of the meaning of work.

So how's your ethical essence??

What Would You Do?

As a police commissioner once said when he turned down the twentieth bribe offer he had received that day, "Ethics ain't easy!" All of us are faced by those moments when doing what's right is very different from doing what's easy or what would be the most profitable. That's one of the reasons a company needs to have a mission statement or a code of conduct: so that employees understand what's expected of them when they're faced with the choice between right versus easy, ethical versus profitable.

The problem is that so many choices fall into the grey area in between! What do you do when making the ethical choice will almost certainly hurt someone? What if doing something a little bit wrong will help create a very large "right"? Take a few moments to read the examples below and answer the questions they pose, and you'll see what I mean.

- Your co-worker asks you to cover for him so he can sneak out of work early to go to his son's softball game. Do you agree? If he went anyway, would you keep silent, especially if you knew most of your co-workers would consider you a snitch or a prude or a "goody-two-shoes" for speaking up

- You're about ready to sign a big new client to a contract worth over $50,000. Your boss is under a lot of pressure to increase sales. He calls you into his office and tells you his job is on the line, and he asks you to include the revenue for your contract in the sales figures for the quarter that ends tomorrow. You know the contract is a sure thing but the client is out of town and cannot possibly sign by tomorrow. What do you do?

- The manufacturing cost of the widgets your company makes has dropped by 50%. One of your customers, Sam, tells you he knows this because he is best friends with your company's VP of production, and asks you for a discount on his order. Your boss okays the discount. Your other customer, Sue (who is one of your best friends and knows nothing about the drop in manufacturing costs) places the exact same order for widgets as Sam. Do you offer her a similar discount? Do you tell her about the drop in manufacturing costs?

- Company policy forbids co-workers to become romantically involved. You go to the same church as someone from another department, and you find yourself becoming attracted to this person. Do you pursue the relationship?

- Your best friend is the VP of one of the companies with which your firm does business. You take her out for lunch just to catch up on personal stuff, and you pick up the check. Do you declare this a "business lunch" and submit the receipt for reimbursement?

- While in the restroom, you overhear your boss telling a colleague that Bob is going to be laid off at the end of the quarter, in about two weeks' time. Bob is a good friend of yours. Do you tell him?

- One of the newest salespeople in your division is a real goof-off, never showing up for work on time, distracting other people with his antics, and so on. You complain about him to your boss, who tells you the kid is the son of the company president. Your boss instructs you not only to leave the new guy alone but also to make his sales numbers look good by throwing him some no-brainer accounts. What do you do?

Now, just in case you're feeling very virtuous because you *know* you'd always make the ethical choice in those cases, ask yourself:

Have you ever:

> ... lied to your mother? your boss? the IRS?
>
> ... lied so you wouldn't hurt someone's feelings?
>
> ... lied to get out of a business or social engagement?
>
> ... taken a questionable deduction on your income tax?
>
> ... fudged figures on a report to make the results look better?
>
> ... taken a sick day when you weren't sick?
>
> ... lied to a customer ("we sent your order yesterday") or creditor ("the check's in the mail")?
>
> ... cut corners on quality control?

... blamed someone else for something you knew you were partly responsible for?

... used any of these phrases: "Everybody does it," "It's the lesser of two evils," "It's only a little white lie," "It doesn't hurt anyone," "Who will know?"

... put inappropriate pressure on others?

In the real world, ethics ain't easy. Somehow we need to come up with a way of looking at even the most complicated situations and evaluating them with an eye to what's right—not what will cause the least trouble. We need a basis upon which to build the kind of success that feels good because we know what we're doing represents us at our best. Coming up with this solution means being willing to confront the culture we now work with. How far are you willing to go to be ethical?

Why are companies slow to deal with leaders who fail?

With more reports about ethics/compliance issues multi-billion dollar fines being paid out shouldn't these companies hold their leadership accountable for the decision that caused these issues?

What's the problem here? Aren't leaders supposed to:

- Set the tone for the work environment to be one that is positive, inclusive and empowering.

- Model the behavior they want others to emulate.

- Be the change they want others to embrace.

- Live the values they preach, promote and expect others to do the same.

If they don't do these, why keep them?

How many chances should a leader of any organization have when they have done something wrong i.e. illegal, etc? How many? When these leaders are kept on board, doesn't anyone see what happens to the morale of the employees? Don't they understand that customers, both present and future are watching what happens to resolve these situations? Is it the legal process that keeps them in power? If so, what does that say about the effectiveness and the value of compliance training? I wonder if senior execs participate in their organizations compliance training program? Certainly one can be unethical and yet complaint right?

Aren't all employees expected to play by the same rules? If mid level leaders were to have done serious harm to the company would there be the same hesitancy to deal with them, or would they be dealt with immediately? Shouldn't the "no exception" rule apply to ALL employees? In addition, what does this tell employees about the importance of all their compliance and ethics training when no one is held accountable?

And where does ethics come into play in situations like these? How often is the term ethics used with a leader's wrongdoing? Why not? Because how do you prosecute someone for being unethical?

I just don't get it.

A NOTE BEFORE I LEAVE YOU

Well, there you have it—Ideas, research, insights, wisdom, and tools to help you build trust as a pathway to ethics, ethical behavior, and the importance of strong ethical leadership. I hope you found a few "nuggets" or an "Ah-ha" moment or two that caused you to stop, think and start to implement in your organization. Who can argue about the importance of maintaining a good reputation?

The development of trust leads to loyalty. It also helps you own your moral compass and act on it regularly. From here you can continue daily to build the value of accountability and the importance of creating a strong commitment to the advancement of ethical leadership. Until next time, I wish you all the best.

ABOUT THE AUTHOR

Thank you for taking the time and making the commitment to reading this leadership series. Hopefully, there were a number "nuggets" that helped you think in a uniquely different way about the role and purpose of leadership and ethics. I also hope that the tools and insights I shared will help you create a truly exceptional workplace.

Frank C. Bucaro, CSP, CPAE
Values-Based Leadership Expert
Frank C. Bucaro and Associates, Inc.
630-483-2276

Also check out my values-based, leadership and business ethics programs that:

- Strengthen organizations by decreasing the odds of an ethical/compliance violation.
- Energize and motivate participants to understand the value of consistent "high road" behavior.

• Support the individual and the organization in contributing to the company's success through values-based leadership development.

For more information about the above program or one I can tailor make for your organization, visit my website at www.frankbucaro.com.

FINAL NOTE

Thank you so much for reading my book. I hope you really liked it.

As you probably know, many people look at the reviews on Amazon before they decide to purchase a book.

If you liked the book, **could you please take a minute** to leave a review with your feedback on Amazon, Goodreads or both?

A few minutes is all I'm asking for, and it would mean the world to me.

Thank you so much,

Frank Bucaro

Made in the USA
Coppell, TX
06 August 2021